THE

ZOO

IN

WINTER

selected poems

POLINA BARSKOVA

Selected and translated by Boris Dralyuk and David Stromberg

MELVILLEHOUSE

BROOKLYN, NEW YORK

The Zoo in Winter: Collected Poems

© 2010 Polina Barskova

Translation © 2010 Boris Dralyuk and David Stromberg

The following translations in this book first appeared in other publications:
"Ariel's Message," "Farewell to the Ghost," and "Scene" in *Cardinal Points*
"Happiness" in *Two Lines Online*
"Madeness" in *Ulbandus*

First Melville House printing: January 2011

Melville House Publishing
145 Plymouth Street
Brooklyn, NY 11201
www.mhpbooks.com

ISBN: 978-1-935554-26-4

Printed in the United States of America

1 2 3 4 5 6 7 8 9 10

Library of Congress Cataloging-in-Publication Data

Barskova, Polina.
[Poems. English Selections]
The zoo in winter : collected poems / Polina Barskova ; translated from Russian and edited by Boris Dralyuk and David Stromberg.
    p. cm.
Includes bibliographical references.
ISBN 978-1-935554-26-4
1. Barskova, Polina--Translations into English. I. Dralyuk, Boris. II. Stromberg, David, 1980- III. Title.
PG3479.R747A2 2010
891.71'5--dc22

                    2010046823

O garden! Where the swan's black gaze,
which so resembles winter...

—VELIMIR KHLEBNIKOV, "MENAGERIE"

CONTENTS

Polina Barskova is commonly regarded as the finest Russian poet under the age of forty working today. She is widely admired for her graceful riffs on poetic modes and forms. The light, playful quality of her verse counterpoints its emotional and intellectual gravity. Like Lou Salomé, the heroine of one of her recent poems, Barskova is a "tightrope-walker" who expertly flirts with and skirts convention, always making it look "so simple." But there is nothing simple about her art.

Russian poetry is notoriously self-reflective, but as the commentaries that accompany this volume attest, rendering a collection of Barskova's densely allusive verse required especially great vigilance. One may say that, as an inheritor of both the modern and postmodern traditions, Barskova regards words as serious playthings. Her poems incorporate and respond to a variety of voices – from friends to great poetic predecessors. This can be seen, for example, in her long poem "War," which incorporates portions of lesser known lyrics by Russia's beloved poet, Aleksandr Pushkin. Doing justice to her poems meant carrying her allusions and puns across the linguistic threshold of English, stretching the language as far as it would go.

Like Anna Akhmatova, Joseph Brodsky, and Vladimir Nabokov – the great Russian authors whom she admires and elegizes in this collection – Barskova is steeped in her native culture's literary tradition. And like them, she is also profoundly engaged with other literary traditions. Her poems teem with striking and irreverent classical allusions, and reflect her career-long involvement with the works of Shakespeare. Since her move to the U.S. in 2000, Barskova's poems have further developed an American strain. Her most recent poems are steeped in her experience of both the East and West coasts of the U.S., and reverberate with echoes of Elizabeth Bishop.

Barskova is also a master of poetic forms, ranging from the most rigidly precise iambic tetrameters to rhythmic free verse. She uses these forms to supply and bolster the semantics of her verse. The metaphysical conceit of "Happiness," for instance, relies on a tight prosodic structure of alternating rhymes that loosens toward the middle and firms up – and reaffirms – toward the end. Remaining faithful to these forms in English was both a challenge and a thrill.

In selecting the seventy-nine poems in *The Zoo in Winter*, we wished to present Barskova in all her moods – passionate and analytical, rapturous and cool, profoundly serious and daringly flippant. We were also exceedingly lucky to get expert help: Polina Barskova – who teaches Russian literature at Hampshire College – collaborated closely with us on every translation. Selecting from her seven Russian-language collections as well as from her more recent work, we looked for poems that lent themselves to translation and were most representative of the poet's diverse achievements. With these criteria in mind, we set upon our joint effort to introduce, with utmost fidelity, the depth and range of Polina Barskova's artistic output for the English reader.

Boris Dralyuk and David Stromberg

FROM

A SQUEAMISH RACE

(1993)

I will not kill myself.
Out of disgust, ineptness.
I'm hoping for a pleasant death
Which loves me as you do, my amethyst birdy.
You'll posthumously understand that I
Am the result of multiplying
Coleridge by Leningrad,
Snow by an orange,
A foe by a friend.

All that'll happen to me
Is better than what has already.
The endless tango of trams traveling backward.
The merging of the market with the plant "Electropower"
Awakes the wish to laugh and draw.

All who'll be with me
Are kinder than you are, more clean.
And so it's in vain that you live with me.

And up above us quake the hands, huge and obscene,
Of our hopeless homeland, Great and Unearthly.

CEMETERY AT KOMAROVO

(not far from the grave of Akhmatova)

The bass strings of red pines.
The Chinese eyes of a dazed squirrel.
Far-off, a shuttlecock flies up
                    an acrobatic underskirt.
A children's bedroom. Little beds
               and night-lights.
A tombstone, through the feathered forelock
Of gray moss, looks upon the others.
Warm needles, made of copper, steel –
Mosquitoes with a long and vicious stinger.
Smells of an outhouse, of decay, of fire.
Next to the honored corpse another's death has faded.
I tear the pantleg and mash up the glass.
Away with you, portrayal of an inglorious interior!
A squirrel's pink flare, the righteous ire of a terrier.
Don't trust your secrets to your journals or to children.
You will offend the proud dead with these acts.
Do not chase down the poison pill with juice.
One living in a cemetery is ashamed and lonely.

"Here lies one whose name was writ in water"

A dispassionate witness – a leech
Lodged on a dead brown branch –
Recalls a morning like the viscous yolk of praise.
The children silently descended to the riverbank to fill their rancid flasks.
Their footprints in the sand were shallowish and small.
A boy in a soiled shirt inhaled the chatter of the heat,
The foretaste of the evening with a wet scar on its cheek.
The lithe boy palpated the sky in lemon bruises, the graven
Decoration of the Earth. Only the salt rash on his temple
Betrayed the work of glands, only the militant luster of fever
In the turquoise eyes, the straining of the darkened forehead,
And the indifferent rows of identical waves
Spoke of how drearily-banal fate is.
Plunging towards the bottom he had neither twisted nor fought back,
He wanted only death.
What matter is brief pain?
He watched the glimmer of the yellow spots of sky
And with his lips caught the blue beans of bubbles.
One cannot live.
                    And nobody will ever pay the costs
Of sheets, books, condoms, fences.
Humility will neither help nor cure
And everything around one causes suffering maddens strangles cripples
A guileless birth. But memory is not excused
Absorbing the interlocutor's pupil, I wasn't able to deceive
And the world choked on this
                    Coughing loudly.
Poplar cotton.
                Snowdrift. Snowdrift. Snowdrift.

Cities are all alike all over.
Full of garbage cans and hold-ups.
Sometimes a family of hermaphrodites
Goes out of town to play volleyball and dice.
And on wet sand their little dogs
Bite their own tails with mounting anger.

Two adolescents in their designated buildings
See one another in a common obscene dream.
A coffee wreath of dates
Remains suspended on a fattened moon.

Our suffering would fill up tanks,
Dishes, cartons, containers, and bags.
Would smooth out all the cavities and bumps
On faces gutted out by smallpox. Waffle cones
Will fly up, giving off such sounds, that blameless
Virgins will be locked in dungeons by their brothers,
That gondolas of closeness start to crawl
Through the canal of distance. Shriveled hands
And hairdos twisted into snapdragons.

The earth, the snow: rock salt with cinnamon.
After the terrorists' visit, the kitchen is ashen.
We are reflected in a puddle with no bottom,
You abrade space with a coarse mitten.

The darkened scabs of cherries
Beneath the night-light's yellow stream.
Magpies nervously croak.
Puppies quietly grunt.
From the tip of the mainland,
Through sourish waves,
You see the breathing, melting
Lunar islets.

Perched on a tongue by the sea,
You sense at your elbow
A watchful pendulum
And an insulted oboe.

The illusion of loneliness
Is like a soaked-through fleece.
You hear a seabird howl,
Your bracelet cuts into your wrist.

When the best graphomaniacs ruin
Their parquet floors with paraffin,
And bristle at their servants: "No! Enough! Begone!" –
Inventing the color of vodka, the smell of Mary Jane,

Above the cover of the sea gather the experts
Of this life. All their apologies are curt.
Confessions, curt.
Their jokes bedevil, like the demon at the tail end of the bottle.
Their tears drag to the bottom, into lime captivity.
It's only here that you can get up on your knees and never get up off your
    knees,
Having, for it, no reasonable cause and downy bedding.

They're bound together by the ancient, shameful torment
Of bitter mischief, naive mettle.
With them, you become strong, short-sighted.
You hear the puppy fall asleep, the leafage rattle.

Everyone's abandoned me?
               Well, then, I'll just be a seed.
I'll gnaw straight through the burnt-up firmament.
The last age has arrived.
And this will be the time,
In which the word becomes lament.
It's not the age of love, which covers
The nothingness under the wig of sin.
It is the age of truth, which cannot hear.
It is the age of light and soaring verse,
Which is delirious, but doesn't dwindle.
Will it have everything? No! It will not have us.
The weak world will be colored by a different foulness.
In the beloved's hand sometime before the dawn
Will flutter, then, the curls Holofernes.

A heap of gypsies. The minty smell of scalded birch-brooms.
A hen vendetta, fights, reprisals, payoff
For a foolish shooting-range with Eros's thin laughter,
The fact that yawns and penicillin will remain
From the word "dear", which is as meaningless as abstinence.
Here, everyone is St. Sebastian. Thin laughter scatters
Over the sea and dale and dale and sea again.
For the fact that powerless happiness merges with sorrow,
Whose name one finds in a newspaper's dirty small print.
Soldiers! do not drink rain from trenches, do not gnaw your biscuits.
Bemoan the dead Apollinaire, who worked your bullfight.
Soldiers! green freshwater fish: trout, mackerel, horse mackerel.
Soldiers! girlfriends of pug-nosed Mars, a toothless pack.
You're tough meat, soldiers! smoked meat.
But how soon it came…
They'll cover her round-breasted carcass with nets.
She's unafraid of shame.
I'll make her a gift of my life-wallet-trinket.
But how soon it came…
A thievishly-imperishable table has arisen:
Neither a bed, nor lodge.
How soon approach the wretched sisters of the Universe
And how alike they are.

Chorus: *This above all: to thine own self be true,*
And it must follow, as the night the day,
Thou canst not then be false to any man.

I still recall the eyes: two cooled sores on a cooling body.
Still see the fluttering of those short-fingered hands:
The agony of junkyard pigeons.
Behind him crawled the interlacing shades of
Those swallowed by the quenchless Chronos.

The torn spine of a window. Past it, talcum-powdered,
Is a sloping wasteland. An unprimed canvas.
Not far off lies a park. Above the park there hangs
A Ferris wheel, the bridge nearest to God.
It seems I shiver at the lavishness of wishes,
The beads of nicotine that fly above my head.
The pendulum has grown confused in the monotony of oscillations
Between the red and white, the treacheries and treasury.

When you betray yourself, you must remember why
You have entrusted your own fate to life,
And that the camel keeps a store of hope within his hump,
And that your enemy's the sparkling orator, but I alone, I am your friend –
        the bore.
And that the skilled magician can't bring off a miracle.
And that you're loved by relatives, of whom you've had your fill.
And she alone deceives you. Rotten and depraved.

Chorus: *Cut off even in the blossoms of my sin,*
   Unhouseled, disappointed, unaneled,
   No reck'ning made, but sent to my account
   With all my imperfections on my head.

A bird appeared to me this morning
With a barbed wire in its beak.
In the immeasurable stronghold,
The beasts have stilled. I glumly spat
In the already troubled waters –
My spittle swam towards the West.
O welcome news! You did not rush!
I'd heard so very much about you
When overripe clusters of cherries
Were lost at the first hint of daybreak,
When fog streamed in across the sea
And down
     Starch-stiffened folds.
Well, then, I'll only wash the mildew
Off my face. All will be well.
I did not sin. The reason being –
My concubine had been a single
Hollow and spotless bit of cinder.
She does not smell of carrion, like any living flesh…
And with this punitive forgiveness the Lord has now assessed my choice.
O welcome news! How you are dreadful.
There's not a bit of sanctity in you.
I'm but a middling puritan.
But you're a purse riddled with holes.
Again I am a beggar. I'll be forced
To foster deserts the entire age.

The rainbow crumbles in my dream.
Light grows, just like the bosom of a goddess.

11

Chorus: *Her garments, spread about, drove her like a nymph.*
　　　　　Amidst all this she sang snippets of songs,
　　　　　As if she hadn't felt disaster.

It is no longer evening, not yet night.
And the horizon spills across the flannel.
When a few letters do not represent
The meanwhile otherworldly snowfall,
Nor the hillock, which befits a cat
Much more than it befits... nor Lethe,
In which all rosy braggarts aim to bathe
Themselves, one following the other,
Then it is death. Death has surrounded us.
We hide like foxes in a burrow neath an elm.
And we can only to suck the eyes out
From ironbound-angular hunters.
When a few letters do not represent
The lantern, drilling through the stratosphere,
And not at all, at all, what you conceive,
Then it, I dare to utter it, is love.
And to repeat it. Swallow it for ages.
When a few letters represent both this,
That, and the other. And you as well, choleric one protected by string music,
Then we are dealing with the godly. With poetry, both cynical and clumsy.
Hearts of Australia, of Europe, both Americas
Outstretch themselves, now, aiming to grab hold.
Oh what a horse: the legs, the neck, the stature,
How black it is. I thank you humbly,
My one and only, unattainable and so forth.
Cupid is choking on cold barley porridge.
Venus now feels the softness of the turf.
It's not yet morning. But it is no longer night.

Chorus: *Why, man, they did make love to this employment.*

They pierced the hat with one stroke of a peacock
Feather. And tossed it underneath the table.
O, who would know where I had gone last night?
Why, in the end, did I wind up at the cathedral?
Why did I gawk at the old scrawny men, huddled beneath the cataracts of
      icons…

I prodded with a boot the trembling tuft
Of shadows. Almost like windfalls in a garden.
I do not think that I came after her.
It is from her. It is from her I go.
In vain did I appear before a foreign god,
Urging myself with someone else's decency.
Even the weather has turned out to be
Repulsive in December's tapestry.

A fool interrogates: the background is mixed-up.
But so it goes: the gender is mixed-up.
A pair of old men who wear corals in their ears,
But neither of whom has a tongue.
The mole is piling dirt on Thumbelina.
The word zealously burns the people's hearts.
Having rejected God, he turns back to the church.
What can be done, then, if the world is such.

Chorus: *But heaven hath pleased it so,*
To punish me with this and this with me.

Who brought me through the weeping of a gray lagoon.
Who shivered, when I froze.
Who remained silent, when there weren't words enough for two.

The sobbing of the ferry terminal's bleak shutters.
The long oars' turgid strings.
The wormwood clots of metal play beneath the water,
Turning to soporifics: warm complaisant smoke.

Where is that pliant laughter.
It ran, like an echo, ahead.
Where is that thorny voice –
A grotto sprayed with azure,
Where we could meet, not shamed that
Our palms were drenched in sweat.
Where is his tinny heart,
Refracting fuss.

Could it really have vanished in catacombs of poisoned water?
Like a ruby ringlet forming at the lips –
You have shot through his stomach.

See, a somber mark
Has spread across the faded jeans.
Death's a reliable cell.
We'll wind up there together.

Chorus: *Since my dear soul was mistress of her choice*
And could of men distinguish, her election
Hath seal'd thee for herself.

Where the lake of frozen cream of wheat
Is speckled with spiders' tracks.
Where – slightly swollen, delicately pale – your profile
Was like a sorrowfully falling leaf.
Where, in the night, an earth-bound safe exploded,
Strewing about the bluish constellations.
And where a fir fluttered its fingers, swaying
And swearing, like a tired pianist.

It should be there. Sappho, with her face pressed
Into her sharp and rubber knees,
Whispered of how she could have loved me
If it were not for nature's obstacles.
There, where the bed with metal netting stood,
And where our jackets dried on radiators.
And where we dreamt the sharp smell of our school.
Venice and wintry Moscow.

If only I'd not injure others with my imitation,
Though my arrows do not reach their end.
If only I'd only not maim myself with diligence
In the fanned threading of poetic lines…

Sensitivity and sensuality are not
Too similar. Cover the window with your coat,
And close your eyes, and stop your ears with a soft wax,
So that, with the humility of an orphan,

You weep and remain silent during the confession.
But no! Farewell. Do not attempt to find me.
Let, then, the fool call you a sweetheart.
Let, then, the postman soar high above Europe.
My love for you is more forlorn than lichen.

Chorus: *My tongue and soul in this be hypocrites;*
How in my words soever she be shent.

Love is schizophrenia. You asked me then, doctor, what I was reading.
I was nine. It wasn't worth the work to reconcile me with reason.

Attempt to find a white transparent sheet.
Since, doctor, the Creator's not at all an eye,
All that I'm yet to see will not be to your liking.
I now perform my fate, switching the octave.
And I admit, one hears a motley banal wheeze:
This is a ruddy angel stuck to iron by his wing,
And dangling now beneath a famous arch,
Emitting nectar, beer, and diesel fuel.
It's good that love is always an advance,
And few can make it stretch till payday.
Because of them, the marble patches gape,
At Komarovo, for example. That's the balance.

My author had repulsive penmanship.
And furthermore, many untimely periods.
Can he who doesn't love eternity be loved?
Soon I'll take up that question.
Oceans of words, which I command to them,
Will swell like foam onto the monitor.
Refer to numbers, other languages, and colors,
But do not bend these words to change.
Remember the Udelnaia, the ashy snow? And there,
The doctor's dark lips in complacent froth.
If I go mad into the blaze of graphomania,
He has no power to burst through the trembling gate
Of disaffection. Incidentally, it is winter.
Just the right time to read the "Iliad" again.

Chorus: *That he is mad, 'tis true:*
  'Tis true 'tis pity;
  And pity 'tis 'tis true.

A verse is open space. And nothing more.
If you look down, you're mired in a muddled mystery.
If you give up the smallest part to mutual friends,
They'll tear it all away, leaving no stone unturned.
So you'd do well to shut my mouth up with a sneer.

What good, stooped mage, is your swamp fire here,
When up above us throbs this chandelier.
I won't make peace with you, o hallowed harmony.
I've left too many tracks
In this cramped little paradise of branded soul,
Something's forever slandered in your bellows.
This can't be grasped. And a great drought
Comes over every mindful person.

In part, it is this snob. This royal city.
Where on Liteyny Avenue's a house - a monument to Roman madams.
A megalopolis, sleeping in underthings
Beneath the unreliable protection of an ornate fence.

If I could somehow bring it to its knees,
Somehow get rid of it. All hopes are dashed.
Do not make claims. Wipe off your face. The final slave alone
Will be the final victim of the fleeing seraphim.

Chorus: I do not set my life at a pin's fee;
       And for my soul, what can it do to that,
       Being a thing immortal as itself?
       It waves me forth again: I'll follow it.

To master weeping without tears. Then it is easy.
Outside, snow bubbles like a glass of Veuve Clicquot.
The cat bats at a nightmare with a fleshy paw.
And what temptation: asphalt, the fourth floor.
Someone was rescued just in time by a Lepage
From the most shameful circle of a backwoods hell.
If you could swim up from the depths of the Dead Sea
And find – Fanfan – the very highest haystack,
And chew on straw, turning your face toward the sunset.

If the crow's cry did not disturb the people's hearing.
If death could truly seal the viscious circle.
If man weren't able to snuff out the icon-lamp.

FROM
        EVRIDEI AND ORPHICA

        (2000)

recovers from sleep – forces open her eyes –
opens a book of poems –
pushes off from the bottom of thoughtlessness with an intellectual pole –
the poem ends quickly – she stares at the date.
This happened in 1976:
The blessed wild Muse
Gave herself to a soldier
Of the wonderful front. And the child swam
In a laurel-leaf basket down the famous river,
That is, down Lethe, trembling, panting,
As do all wronged people.
And then – miraculous salvation, great deeds, hundreds of eyes
Digging these letters like a holey tooth
For a root canal, which would unite us,
Haggard readers, with pulsating glory.
The poem gave itself to anyone, writhing, wagging its tail;
Just like the devil in tumbler, trembling, tempting.
One bare Saturday morning it acquired me,
Who too was born in nineteen hundred and seventy six.
We were as clearly and offensively unequal
As a chopper – and a butterfly, a tulip – and onion soup.
The poem was like a bubble that had risen from the depths,
From lips that have released the final word.
The poem was a sacred mountain, and I sat below it,
Enjoying the scenery, having removed my heavy boots,
While it, the size of an avalanche, rolled down a tear,
Condemning me to an nobly-sweet death in a duel
With the indifferent natural force of words arranged by someone
The force which erases the lives of persons and nations,
So that the period and the apostrophe stand always,
So Shakespeare hollers, Horace remains silent.

You are a black hole in my armor,
You're the Achilles, phantom heel of a poor cripple
Who, with the greased shoves of his hands,
Directs his way toward a beer stand.
We wander along Kamennoostrovskii Prospekt on a dwindling-summer
    day
And, as a bridegroom nears the bridal tent, we near an open-armed
    delicatessen.
For you? What else but cheese and wine.
For me, a few plums and a lot of meat.
And we will sit at the resounding window
Until the pseudo-morning hour.
And I will watch as you grow slowly drunk,
And intersperse your voice with hackneyed notes,
And iridesce, from strand to strand, with hair that is no longer
Copper, not yet silver. So why are you
So crudely precious to my makeup,
Where I admit you, sole among the living,
And so equate you with the ones who have, there in the tear-
Inducing smoke of dreams, already gathered in a flock?

I. The Poet Khlopushkin

I recall walking in, him sitting on the bed
Bloated and horrible (lord, rub it out!
These recollections are wholly ill-timed –
Write, little slattern, about what's inside).

And I recall his port voice thundering –
He'd be a chorister, had he not been a Jew –
When, as in Delphi, the truth struggled through
His mouth, eaten away by verbiage.

The god of vanity, the gaudy Buddha
Of Chinese shops, the miracle of sales,
But if you listen in – perhaps… it could have…
But no… It can't be – sleight of hand, mirage.

It cannot be that this runaway clown,
That this emeritus Pantagruel
Who on white paper sits morosely-brown,
Prevailing over third-rate drunkenness

Looked at the world like a mouse at a cat's snout –
In his concluding, slightly freezing sweat,
And winked at it, like Faust at the devil,
When it begins to reek of fire from afar.

Now grasping that the cards are stacked against him,
His *marriage* as useful as a dead man's treat,
He keeps on gasping out: "Ligeia, Seraphita",
And lines of verse decay from their resale,

But something in them (let us say, a comma)
Does not succumb to the decay, and look –
It flies like interference in night's ether
And whispers: "You're eternal, my dear freak…"

II. The Poet Pliushkin

We fought through the hot punch of winter nights,
And through the whipcord of June's steely torrents,
He tracked me everywhere, as if he were the moon.

With a bat's visage and the body of a capon,
He must have been the only one to whom
I didn't vow in pimply greed's raw daze: "I'll come!" –
Nothing in him could have ignited a young girl.

And like a logger wears a mitten, the lord wore
Him on his belt – reserved for the most crude
Of literary acts. His word-hoard flared
Up like a butcher shop with crimson, red, and yellow.
He had appeared to me a Flemish still-life –
Embodying the body without any ooh-la-la,
He was a naturalist more trenchant than Zola…

Himself incapable of shades and highlights,
He instantly proofread the verse of others
For the foam's velvetness, the glimmer of the pit,
The bitterness of density, and cried: "a poet!"
"Godly!", "shit!" – And yea his intuition
Never failed him. Just like a jeweler to a diamond,
He drew a sparkling pupil ever closer to a verse
And pulled it, like a fish onto a hook, from non-existence
Up toward himself, giftless and passionless.

Maniac-castrato, he dismembered it in his
Own satin net – the verse died duteously
There… Down in the depths of his weak-sighted eyes.

III. The Poet Peshkin

He was my cherished friend.
We hadn't spoken but a dozen words to one
Another all our lives: he, it appears, was sickened
By my chatter. Slouching, dainty-handed,
He stiffly smoked while leaning on the railing.
Cyanic Virgil led him to a vicious circle:
In Rome he would be Gallus, Orpheus in Thrace,
But he became an idol, here, of lightsome protozoa
And, so as not to lose his mind, taught children.
Like that missionary who smiles in a leprosarium,
Each morning he entered the 11th-grade classroom
And, hearing the answer of a jeering stutterer,
Exhorted himself: "Not a word about fate.
Let books alone have their own fates –
Habent sua fata libelli.
And I? I am a worm-slave. I'm a Chukchi, friend of snows:
I sing all that I see. But why do I see –
Without an icy spring, blueberry shores –
A thick and thickening slurry
Everywhere? Perhaps the Snow Queen's Troll threw something in my eyes?
Perhaps I'm the inheritor of Midas?
Though my all-seeing pain does not transfigure all
To gold, but to a very different mass.
Like a toad from a princess's mouth, my word
Burns no one's heart, but only scatters warts,
While I do battle with it, helpless and nude,
While I hang from it, as a suicide from a noose."

He'd rack himself this way. If he would visit me
Beneath this cherry tree picked clean by squirrels
In this .... town, in this .... country *,
Amid the sirens' wail, the barking of the neighbor's shoot-outs,
In a darker region, then he would sit like this,
Or, maybe, sit like this, and spit his gall
Back at my idle words, resembling a nickel
Squirreled away by a once powerful speech,
But now – an orphan and a town-square whore
Who takes it for a buck and gives it for a fiver.
But her singer lives – a record plays behind the wall,
A picture hangs behind the back – "Samson Torments a Cat"
O yes, her singer lives! The last. The no-account.
The arrogant. The dim. The angry. Why do I waste my words?
Why do I cry? He lives past the grey river
And shovels change into his pocket with a squeamish hand.

* The reader may insert the epithet of his or her choice.

A lonely sail looms black against the background of the sea.
In disappointment, Aegeus tosses his binocular against the cliff,
And having watched the trace of the binocular
Grow planate like a pore amid the waves,
He goes back home and stridently
Proclaims: "All – to the table!"
A lonely sail looms black. Sly Theseus
Stands still, dreams of the throne, mumbles a tango.
And I'm here torturing a little plot, plaited with glory,
And in my depths it's roomy, but not light.
Gone three-tenths of my earthly journey in a circle,
Just like a carousel horse, I repeat to you:
Protect me, your concern, your friend,
Your jovial proviso of preparation for the border.
Cupid's arrow won't reach the middle of
A Californian winter night – and fall into the dark.
Other small gods tickle the back
Of my resistance and your mercy.
While other gods, like gnats in Baltic summer,
Hang over us, a light sphere on thin blueness,
And say: think not of that! cry not of this!
All has flowed off. To muteness – Lethe. To the gulf – along the Neva!

Under a foreign sky, under the ward
Of smiling Berkeley invalids
Whom I attend,
My soul lies like a hero killed,
No longer drawing crows.
Everything toothsome has been pecked from it,
It should be washed by rains and kicked by winds.
But – there is neither rain, nor wind, and one can hardly
Pick out a word to cover up the shame.
Words that serve here are meek and even,
Foreign to past grandiloquence,
That's for the better: how could one describe in Russian
The grand and small (goddamn) details
Of need, so that the martyr's crooked body
Would not be crooked more painfully,
So that, as it had once, it should desire
Purposeless days in place of rueful days?
So that, when it is fed and washed
By me – shirker, upstart, and plague –
It would be one with me,
So that an English-speaking mind's
Plain forces should unite us,
Like, let's say, money, or, let's say, a lie,
When it lies on the blanket,
And you warm its hands and sing.

V. B.

"The stars are hammered in the firmament like nails.
The other planets are akin to fiery leaves.
Meanwhile, the sky rotates about
The Earth, just as a cap about a head."

How does he picture the rotation of a cap?
But then again, philosophers – they're all like that:
They plunder beehives, beaver huts, and nests,
Thwart the astrologers and the occultists,
And count the constellations on a crucified butterfly's wing.

"Air is the start of everything. After it, Earth,
Which is table-like..."

A logical move – paper
Appears together with an inkwell.
What do the ancients' graphomania and childish courage
Promise me?
If one should think, then think about the start of everything,
Peep at the wedding game of Chaos and Order.
("What did they do there, left with nothing?")
"Everything" – "nothing" – this is the sort of drivel
                                                that fills his notebook!

"Planets are burning leaves."

A summer forest fire.
The tears of animals, the smoldering of fatty hides.
A drunk philosopher had strayed into the forest blindly,
And tossed a cigarette butt.

"Stars and nails."

An outright poet-tribune.
Through ages, through the needle's eye
Comes the black thread of metaphor.
Anaximenes wipes his hands on the edge of his t-shirt,
Glances around, furrows his brow, and asks: "Who's here?"

Raymond Radiguet, you and I will today
Each greedily gobble a lone chicken leg,
We'll each, you and I, drink a goblet of wine –
For this, our descendants will pay in due time.
Today is once again your birthday.
We'll decorate the bed with beetroot haulm,
We'll paint our cheeks with beetroot swill,
We'll bring a goat in with a golden beard.
Then – we'll begin to strip each other naked,
Feigning embarrassment and feigning yawns.
And then again, a goblet each of wine –
A stingy country will pay up for this.
Then – you will go off for a long time to the bathroom.
It will grow dark. They'll turn the lights off in the streets.
You will return. The bottle is shamefully empty.
My lips have darkened at the corners.

You pity me, and won't begin to wake me.
But you'll start fuming from a heavy pipe,
And will illuminate me with a stinking match,
Grieving because we just might have conceived
A funny baby on your birthday –
Your son would have been your spitting image, but alive.

It will be long before I wake in soured fumes –
I won't find me and won't find you.
The clothes grow white, the bed grows black –
I'll have to kiss the dead man on the forehead.
Ah, stink of formalin!
Ah, poured-out eye!
Ah, all that's born of us today.

There are no beaten paths along the Way.
He who walk it is alone and in danger.

From Selected Chan Koans

Life gathers over Death like water
Over a stone tossed into it,
And I, crying a senseless NO, will mumble YES,
Collapsing into bliss, forgetfulness.

Yes, dehermeticized, my airplane flies,
Where there is hoar-frost on the window,
My neighbor sleeps immovably,
Providing me the freedom that I need
To look upon a face I do not need,
As on a landscape:

So let the invalid, scaling the porch,
Look from there on a distant beach
And see: serpentine bodies
Glisten, slither,
And women fly, like a bee,
And the stones rustle.

I feel no jealousy, no malice,
Nor others' god-bashing ideas.
Death brought you once to me,
Girl with a puppy,
And now it quickly
Carries you away, to show you off to others.
She has grown tired of delighting cripples

With you: black, golden, naked,
Murderous. *She* wants to entertain
Her peers with your features. And I
Don't so much understand, as do *not*
Not understand: the world of nonexistence
Needs you, and that means I find it
Sympathetic, like that southern home,
From whose porch stares the invalid
Onto a splendid beach,
And with a toothless mouth
Orders the mistress out onto the porch.

Who stands at the closed gates?
Black Eros.
Who's curled his painted lips?
Black Eros.
The rudest of Olympic gods,
A stranger to the soul, rebellious to fate,
He rudely pushes me toward you.
All that's been smelted in me through the years –
The deaf-and-dumb attempts at virtue –
He sends into the thoughtless flames…
I do not need you and you do not count,
What you mean counts a hundredfold.
Black Eros, he's the harbinger of losses,
He stares at us out of the gaping holes
In locks, blindingly blissful at
Our beastliness and brotherhood.
So let him keep his mournful flock
From waking, near him – out of shame,
He'll squeeze it out, as toothpaste from a tube,
Into black holes, into Nothing, into Nowhere.

Volume turns into flatness. Death is this:
A photograph, a plate, or, say, a book.
That against which one flutters like a butterfly,
                              at which one looks,
But not too passionately; to which one speaks, but quietly –
For speech addressed to those who can reflect no light
Will overflow with rhetoric, immediately deaden.
A question, like a forgotten woman, awaits an answer. The answer
Never appears. The woman forgets.
What now, a month later, am I to do with his face,
Glossy and bright, distorted by photographic film –
Which has nothing in common with that dandy and braggart,
But has a lot in common with the "killed in battle" notice?
What? Store it as evidence: HE'D BEEN ONCE, LOOK – HE'D BEEN!
Of course he'd been, just as they say, HE'D BEEN AND GONE.
He'd been a fibber, a petitioner, an atheist, a sage, a moron.
He'd been – salt of the earth, then turned – into a popeyed idol
With the expression of a lack of expression on his face
(An expression must change). While photo-ice-floes –
Are mere reproaches for the gift of sight, which fastens on a dead man
Who's probably already eyeless underneath a layer of clay.

We were reflected in a piano, in someone else's flat,
And you said to me, laughing: Look there, look there,
How awe-stricken and meekly lie four
Unbright bodies: two outside, two inside.

I turned to the reflection, braced on my elbow,
Splitting my stiff movement in two,
While in the piano... A scorched antique portico
Tinged a couple's concerns with a flame's memory.

Head thrown back, you laughed, forgetting why.
Your laugh bounced like a ball among shadows.
And I, hugging you, watched as into the chasm
We go. And the further, the deeper, the darker the lacquer.

FROM

ARIAS

(2001)

For Nina Samus

each time I try to complain to someone about life
someone's inevitably irritated
how dare you young healthy beautiful
and my interlocutor doesn't even guess
that these three words affect me
like abracadabra affects a pumpkin
or rather like midnight affects Cinderella's carriage
I lose all touch with reality
and come rolling with a crash down the stairs
pouring out orange innards
permeated with the seeds of reflections
which haunt me like
which simply haunt me
with the persistence of a proper name
let's begin with health
my body seems to me a frosting
a meringue as a sweet-toothed-Gallomaniac would say with a grin
pudgy and blindingly-white on the outside
it's filled with hay-dust
not even fit to be pressed with the teeth
only with gums
a pastry like a frolicsome snow-maiden
a moist cloud
it crawls all by itself into the throat
poof and I'm gone
to my credit one could add
that doctors have not come to an agreement about my illness
they put me on my feet
forced me to dance
and wrote in my medical chart something defiantly illegible
this transition to nervous hieroglyphs

from the exultant calligraphy of a visiting nurse
"skin clean belly soft"
reminds me of the progression of Russian literature
from Nikolai Nekrasov, let's say, to Mirra Lokhvitskaia
neighboring stops you know
but God forbid you'll miss it, nose buried in a book
you'll be lost
youth
my youth
has lasted for a very long time now
and it seems it will continue for a very long time yet
I think inventing relativity
he had in mind precisely the metamorphoses of youth
if a person doesn't tell himself
why I've still got a long way
then he's already dead
and if a man tells you
I'm old
then for the next half-hour
you won't be doing your homework
youth is hyperbole and old age is litotes
and yet it was with the me of today
that the fool Carlos threatened the omnivorous Laura
five or six years have passed
since that confectionery-aromatic night
but gray hair doesn't shine upon my head
my eyelids do not blacken, sinking inward
and I lie evergreen in the cart of a white-eyed black man
a gloomy grandee moralizing a floozy
was punished for his distrust with imperishable youth
they didn't finish talking, judging by everything
that literally chills upon him
but most of all I'm occupied with beauty
I'm driven mad by the fact that the prattle healthyyoungbeautiful
in their language means simply alive

that is, one like us, one of us, not another
call Oscar
let him crawl up, clanging his shackles
he'll puke a green carnation from his innumerably used lips
you ought to be ashamed to call me beautiful
in doing so you castrate beauty
no longer does she leap from the balcony into green twilight
nor return near morning, wet and stinking with a frog in her teeth
no
she begins to resemble her master
she informs on him to his young wife
while he wipes his boots in the hallway
she finishes his supper
I'd always placed myself outside the brackets of beauty
multiply it by not mixing with it
I tried to be born of the most beautiful of mothers
so as to scan for years
her nearly ethereal monkey hands
her pink hair
I shrink with pleasure
introducing her to my friends
observing as their glances dart in a panic
from her to me and again to her
and grow calm there, like an agitated child
are you sure that this is your mother
a neighbor famed for his tactfulness
plaintively asked me
together we can serve
as a textbook allegory for degeneracy
a gas station on the ruins of the Acropolis
I'm proud of my destiny to highlight her radiance
I was guided by the same principle
in selecting the lifelong addressee of my dedications
this slightly spoiled our
as he expressed it

faire l'amour
like all inveterate adulterers
he was excessively fastidious with words
in the dialect native to both of us
he never could find anything
that wouldn't make this, well, you know
in one way or another laughable
that wouldn't alienate darken mangle
but would simply express it depictingly
that would serve in relation to the object as simply a window
and not as the eye of a camera, squinting with the consciousness of power
     over this object
a word
when we made love
his beauty somewhat distracted me
and likewise it didn't fully satisfy me
to possess this beauty undividedly
but what a joy it was to observe
as another victim would divide
into a remainder of common sense
lout vulgarian rogue
and the urgent need
to unite with him in the bathroom
while I and the puzzled lawful companion of the other victim
discuss the reproduction of Munch in the living room
one can talk a long time about Munch
when they returned
I felt myself the victor
and not him
who was already not quite able to distinguish defeat from victory
and not her
who was swept off like Dorothy from Kansas by a fairy-tale tornardo
and anticipating explanations with Toto
I felt the delight of Pygmalion
upon learning that Galatea had received an A in painting

all these delights did not last long
giving way to tenderness
what a good girl I was
that in the pitch-black darkness of the final shudder
as the simple-hearted Aleksandr Kushner could so easily have said, if he
     hadn't already
to the cynical Fedor Tiutchev
I spied and remembered
remembered forever
the arrangement of six hacked-up bodies on the floor
a young newlywed bride
but the hooves already clapped upon the castle bridge
and the blue beard fluttered
her brothers saved
the poor little one, unlike myself
a late and only child
and now with an unusual sluggishness
I savor my recollections
like my girlfriend Katia
who ate the same banana
a rarity in the Soviet jungle
in the night for two months straight
letting the darkening little body rest from the torture
under a pillow in the daytime
but my problem is more pressing
I'll have to stretch my sweet fruit
till the end of my days
and here I have something to brag about
6 hours and 42 minutes of the dank evening of October 10, 1996
when he went to the kitchen to fetch an ashtray
and froze in the doorway
across from a lamp turned indignantly around
letting me get my fill in abundance
of his profile, unexpected in every curve
I managed to last a month and a half

I rolled down the nose unforgivably quickly
a crazy childhood habit showed
with a scream that chilled my daddy's soul
of sliding on my stomach down the icy bunker
of the monument to the heroes of the Leningrad Blockade
but with the lips I didn't make that blunder
like a selfless Lilliputian
I slinked across my Gulliver
skirting the ice-holes of pores
forcing my way through the brutal thickets of bristle
so as to bury myself finally in the native flesh
and to inhale the alcoholic-nicotinic fumes
I was filled with this spirit as a balloon is filled with helium
which gave me the opportunity
to rise slightly above the terrain
and survey it from above
one could still discern the chin
but the Adam's apple was lost entirely over the horizon
so I was left satisfied with this reconnaissance
the journey promises to be a long one
if anything is a shame
it's that I won't reach,
here the Nurse turns red from laughter
and Juliet Montague stops her ears,
the tastiest parts until I'm nearly sixty
though as my gentleman, who's partial to retired quips, would say
alcohol
 – *it's a slow death, but we're not in a hurry*
I've nowhere to hurry
I need to fill
my whole life with his incomparable beauty
which, with his death,
he'd devastated, as locusts had the Principality of Kiev
in the *Tale of Bygone Years*, by the way
this invasion is described with much more authentic bitterness

than in that of the Polovtsy
in all likelihood the chronicler went to into the monastery after
the death of his beloved vegetable patch
I've nowhere to hurry
my route is well known to me
the horses are watered, the guides are sated
the easel's delivered from the Montparnasse basement
where the curly-headed disrober of Anna Gorenko-Gumilev
was kept on brandy and models
and through deception I'd managed to barter
the worn-out butterfly-net from Brian Boyd
so when I complain to someone about life
I don't expect to hear a senseless regret that
I am young healthy and beautiful and that all this is pointless
I expect to hear the laughing "rejoice"
with which you inscribed your book for me
by the way
with the exception of the signature
it turned out to be remarkably mediocre

In the nighttime subway it smelled
Either of narcissi or piss.
You laid your head on my shoulder,
And when a heavy tress
Began to flutter in a fever on the wind,
Then, tucking it behind the ear,
You said: "We'll be getting off soon,
But for now it's good down here."
What's good about this? The sweet shadow
On the cave wall's screen?
We're beautiful and young. More – now
It's obvious we're in
Love with being beautiful and young, and
With dawn in Brooklyn, where
The swollen egg-white of the migrant sun
Has shattered in the boiling water;
With the fact that we cannot enter each other –
So we'll stand in the doorway
And whisper: "You see, it's already five till.
Hurry up, I beg you!"
Just let me hear afresh, just let me see afresh
That blue, that blue, that black.
That slippery Raphaelesque tress
In that scarlet, as usual, mouth.
Let me hear, see, smell, feel, taste,
That cabbage stench – your poverty
And emptiness. For you (like me)
Are absolutely wholly empty.
For this alone, our borders will not meet
Nor our lips merge – a pity –
Twins from Siam, we're fully, nonetheless,

Suited to the nature of things,
Let us not see the ugliness of union, let us not sense
That no bond can be stronger than
That of a tightened, foreign night of babble
And of a milk-cap pressed
Onto a fork, and of the poems your mad father rattles
From memory still. Your splendid chest
In the spirit of Egon Schiele. That senile regret
In the spirit of Afanasii Fet – for fallen youth. And let…
Your temple rest upon my shoulder.

My soul would like to be a pot,
Or rather, what will soon turn out
To be a pot – a lump, a clot
Of bloody-brownish clay. A rout
Of rabid fingers – nabs! – the clay
And – ho! – onto the wheel, the rack,
And starts to rip and mash away
At the unyielding, stubborn block.
But pitying, or grasping that
The carrot's better than the stick,
It daubs the proud clay with a sponge.
The turbid water seeps like juice
And the clay yields beneath it: "Yes…",
Crawling into the palm, as meat
Into a mincer. Eyes are closed.
The pedal smacks. Beneath the hands
A living and warm woe that has
Surrendered to the force of flesh.
But I'm not Doctor Bormenthal,
Nor am I even Mary Shelley.
Of executioners, OBs,
We do not speak. A potter – dash –
He is a potter. He's just hands.
He exists only in the wheel
That's ever twirling. In a primer
He doesn't get past boring B.
He's got no use for cutting C,
To say, of course, nothing of D.
He will impel, he'll breathe, he'll twirl
The wheel, obeying the inferior
Will of the treadle. And the potter,

As one unloved, but much in love,
Through use of primitive enchantments
Invades the tight, the secretive,
And also gently mocking ball,
And it, turn after turn, by fractions,
Having accepted his deception,
Transmogrifies into a pot.
The line moves – and the pot will soon
Be in the furnace, like a youth.
And will turn into – Space, a Thing
Useful to both the bad and good.

The craft that I chose and the craft that chose me
Correlate whimsically… If only! Actually…
Words spread out like the pillow and sheet
In an insomniac's battle. The clay grows like a tumor on a blameless body.
Poetry skims, with a rusty spoon, the foam, cream, fat, the fertile layer
Off the slush of puzzlement accumulated through the day.
Clay is complicit in every action, assumes onto itself my own responsibility,
Holds till the last twitch of the needle, trowel, and sponge.
And most importantly – all this in silence. With that mighty muteness
Which precludes the possibility of not only dia-, but, most importantly –
    monologue.
Hence, from This One ever-seeking-me, I hide, more and more often, in
    That One,
And listen gloatingly to the heavy tread of God:
He searches for me in the streets of Petersburg. In daylight – with a lamp,
And during white nights – with his dogs: Dostoevskii, Gogol, the spaniel-
    Blok.
While I sit, pressing up to the jug's wall, pretending to be wine,
And hope he doesn't fix his potent eye
Into the neck, does not discern down at the bottom
The fore(bond)woman who has run off from his galley,
For when He does bring His lips down to me,
I can discern, through the strong scent of vinegar, the scent of sulfur.
And it's not that a sequence of this kind awakes a bray in me
Of choice, repulsion, misery, or morals,
But if (hello M. B.!) there is an Up above and Down below, I'd like to live
    out here below
The life which has from me been… – from which I have been stolen.
And it is not that I would like to blame someone
(Since, after all, the object and subject of blame are united)
But the clay that pities me and the poetry that consumes me,

Are two things wholly incompatible from vision's point of view.
"Vision" – the name of the last refuge of such
  Reprobates as I, who have deprived themselves of all things other.
  The eye reveals the surface, the finger penetrates the verse,
  The vessel's walls break down, sensing the onslaught of the Word.

With relish, you articulate: "Homo Dicens - nothing."
A turtle might squeak beneath the auto's tire,
A birdy add a bit of red to the rear-view mirror.
Like a cow patty, the plateau spreads
Past the volcano sticking out like the crown of David's head,
Had he stepped into lava.
Sweetly, you focus the tensed lens
On the rusty trident of a cactus, raised up above the herd,
Capturing this instant with a Faustian flash.
You feebly flop with a none too supple backside
Onto the sombrero, which suits you as a saddle
Suits one of the cud-chewing models (to put it lightly).
The heat has a ruinous influence on the rhythmic course of structure.
The camera, like an iguana, shuts its eye.
Speaking Man. Smoking. Reeking. Traveling to a foreign
Land untidily more complicated than
>   Tartu semiotics,
>   Saransk heroics,
>   Venetian wells.
What does the quattrocento feel, dropped back into the Mesozoic?
The condom, even if abundantly lubricated,
Separates the bearer from the abyss, as a parachute.
Again you understand that you – it's you against the background…
Does it really matter of what? And the vultures are waiting.
Not for you. But for you to drive by, and for the acrid blood
Of the armadillo, which (no, did you see that?) is small,
And now looks like a crumpled bathroom mat.
A livid fan of Mexico bursts into the movie theater,
And Prince Charming rushes in a carriage down the stairs.
Watching Man – a museum luxury.
Showing – oh yes!

Even here, where the absence of a viewer attains an absolute.
People, lions, partridges, vultures, and a herd –
All laid themselves under the wheels. All crawled here.
Will you take a picture? I, of course, will.

Gazing at this personage with attentive nipples,
With the face of an old geisha: sharp and blank,
You search its scowl with a metadarwinian quickness
For the denominator of reincarnation. The akyn
Of the zoo staff, the subduer of Rudyard
And darling of French existen… (I can't!),
Has scratched onto the stone that, enveloped by sorrow,
For two years and more, now, this personage won't
Utter "gu-gu", won't toss her ball to the volunteer –
The ramshackle ball in the back right corner.
This is read to me by an inquisitive boy
With guilty squints ("Forgive me, I'm lying").
For two years and more, now, Tarzan hasn't returned
To the lady with the dark-gray face from his crusade.
As Sologub, in empty Petrograd, awaited the ice-out,
The lady baboon awaits the date and monitors the priest
Who daily and irately scratches on the tablet:
Don't give her sugar, it won't help.
For over two years, now – the habits have changed.
Neither hope, nor estrus. On the wall – an ant.
The ball was bequeathed to the overfed rat
Who, in our tragedy, stands in for the nurse.
Agents of metadarwinian quickness make up the choir.
As in a passport photo, unfailingly en face,
The choir sees the lady baboon or, right away, the backs
Of the visitors' heads, departing for the elephant.
And it grows quiet. The rat gnaws on sawdust
Behind the lady baboon's back. She swallows her saliva.

take my head in your hands,
whisper into my ear, all atremble,
as Billie Holiday, ticklishly meowing:
the storm has passed,
and your skull, broken at the neck,
and my skull
will in the near future be inhabited by snakes,
and the youngest will whisper: "slither home"
to her sister, and the eye sockets
will gaze at night, as windows,
into the darkness of the earth,
and the rain's spouts,
seeped through the earth, will begin tapping
against the dark so cozily

so take my head
into your smoked-through,
into your perfumed hands –
it's yours
say: "my sister"
but the jaw can no longer bear the cluster of consonants
and will fall away,
and in that same tap
all will be united – all that's divided us,
that Little Red Riding Hood couldn't bring through the woods

like Billie Holiday, get hung up on this word,
tear into it, as the predacious needle
of the phonograph: my sister, sister!
on Bornholm Island the cat's eye of transgressive
love studied us, squinting from the corner,

my sister
on Bornholm Island, where there is Holiday, where there's a holiday,
where there's a holiday year round –
Day of the Red Taxidermist,
Day of the All-regional Court –
you, into a hand that crumbles,
will take my head and say:
"well, where have you got that Liapkin-Tiapkin?
bring him here!"

FROM
   BRAZILIAN SCENES

   (2005)

1. Carrion-2

Like a terrible beast out of fabulous seas,
A beast cast from regular orders of beasts,
Tossed at night – with no shelter, no right.

This city, it lies, and this city, it rests,
This city, it reeks, and this city, it frets.
A venomous delicate toad.

A black mildew lays waste to the houses of Rio,
And it's forty degrees in the shade due to winter.
And the beauties that haunt shameful quarters –

Are unfailingly beaus. The sweat's pouring down,
Flooding the dam of the overworked frown.
Concourse of lips – black, exhausted.

The sweltering bay's emerald – false and marred –
Is guarded by skinny, cyclopean curs,
And their nurslings are scattered all over

Like the plentiful seeds of some wild, swollen fruit.
The juice sluices out, and the sun boils the spit,
From the ocean – just like cotton candy,

Attacking, the reeking clouds crawl to the bay,
The city's dead-living, like a tooth that gave way,
A shell, overtaken by ants,

Tree of Knowledge, let's say. In the sea, streaks of oil,
Empty bottles (the remnants of tourists).

But the teens go to meet this deplorable wave,
Rushing happily onwards, just as if they've
Not noticed the stench and the trash.

Their bodies are flashing like light little fish,
Like splinters of diamond, shards of water-smoothed glass
Slice the lagoon's upturned palms.

2. Mining of Amethysts in the State of Minas Gerais, Brazil

Do you recall those slaves
Do you recall those bulls
Their oleaginous sweat
Their sweat that's purple-black

Their hunches glisten like bald mounds
The slaves draw flickerings from stone

It's violet it's brown and rose and scarlet
It's heavier than emeralds, flightier than rubies

And gnomes atop the mountain
And gnomes beneath the mountain
Bring it to you
Out of a winding lair

The blind ones will drag out the AMETHYST, and bring it near,
And chain you up in it, just like an ant in amber.
Flickering fire – rattling vessel.
A flaming January, smoldering February.
A miserable town, a land beyond one's grasp.
To come – is one *real*. To leave – another.
A filthy outhouse. A bus station.
It rained and stopped. And rained – and stopped.

Whom can one sympathize with in another land? In one's own?
[Though Trotskii walked in heat, an ice axe found him]

While down here in Brazil a purplish gnome
Caresses cherishes the purplish corpse
Of a small princess. Size of a nutlet? Of a nickel.
The master stands atop the mountain with a gun.
The barrel's purplish pupil widens
Until the bodies down below grow dark beneath the rain

3. Favelas. Children in the Rain

After Elizabeth Bishop

On the slope of a sweltering hill
Children play all day long.
Bespeckled with freckles, a girl
(rescuing shadow, come on!)
And sticking in the sun's eye like a mote, a boy.
With them is a puppy, like a ball of fat in honeyed fluff.
The mongrel, the children – below.
The bulging clouds – above.

The thunder's just about to burst,
And still, the little tramps dig pits,
And still, the little tramps build castles
Using their father's gap-toothed shovel.
The handle's even snapped from it –
There's little sense in such a shovel.
They laugh.… And laughter's tranquil peals
Merge with the threatening thunderclaps.…

O yes! Their peals of laughter
Glimmer like lightning.
They're shorter, straighter than the puppy's yipping,
Struck with rain.
                    Their
Peals of laughter
Like an explosion's echoes
Rocket above the wetted ground.

Meanwhile their mother runs, ridiculous,
                              and fearfully cries out:
Quick, to the house! Quick, to the house!

Look, children – the storm shamelessly
Has sucked your shoes up whole.
Run, children – now in want and roguishness,
The rain's destroyed yours castles, hidey-holes.

But rather, no – the powdery and blackened
Heavy house of rain is roomier,
More dignified than your own hovel.
So it is better – you stay here!
Here, where the rain's translucent glimmering bowl is more
Capacious than the one in which your share of sour milk
                              Is poured.

Susie Sontag's writing about war.
It'd be good for me as well, I guess,
To conceive a Sevastopol tale
And, like Zoshchenko, drink mustard gas.

I cannot. I'd like to – I cannot.
Take Vermeer, now – he had tried to paint
A single earring for a hundred years.
I'm like this, unable to address
Society at large. I am well
Where there is a small hole in the wall,
Where a sock lost in the room,
Like a magnet, draws the gloom.

Derptskii pearls – a yellow earring.
The yellow Russian snows.
Granddad Aleksei Chudinov
Is buried, it appears, in all
Unreality – so Hegel said.
There's no death – so Hegel said.
Only idlers failed to say it.

I do not know.... Whether my gift is
Poor, or I'm morally a fungus
Under the toenail of my people,
Just that I know nothing at all.
I don't know why the Pale Horse guzzles,
So like the half-steed of Münchhausen,
This reddish liquid. It just leaks
From out its backside, colored black,
Pours to the corner where the sock is,

And where your grayish little lock is
Beating atop your pretty head.

My Patroclus, tell me, what shall I do
In this resplendent tent
Upon this flawless hill?

My Patroclus, my famous soldier,
My dusty one, gnawed through with spears!
I do not know. The stars watch over
How you and I live without you.

Hail Malchish, of course.
But what is that to us?
There's no death. Perhaps there isn't.
There's nothing more, there's nothing.

That day the war broke out, that very day.
    —Khodasevich

It's not in vain I dreamt you all
In battle with your shaven heads,
And brandishing your bloody swords,
In pits, high places, on the wall.

Adorno told you very clearly
Writing's shameful living's dreary
If you happen to be certain
That beneath the daily warmth
Like some timber sawed to bits
Like a scattered bunch of seeds
There lie bodies that are hollow
On the surface of the earth

Out of them the spirit's – bust
They give off but stink and dust
Between them wander pairs
Of audacious crows

Awake, oh timid one!
Deep in your cave
The holy lantern
Burns until morn.

I woke up near evening
And went for a walk
The moon rocked
In the lilac sky
Struck with the strong

Solution of rain
The flowers had fluttered
Down at the ground
Like the first word
Of newborn love
They sounded
Piercingly-new
And moved slowly
Like the fires
Of funeral processions
In days long ago

But I fear: that midst the clashes
You will squander for all time
The coy meekness of your motions,
Charm of tenderness and shame.

A soldier hears a soldier say
You see I'm burning out
I'll be no more by end of day
Come on and love me now

Then the soldier answers back
You are lost my friend
For farewell merriments you have
Neither gums nor hands

All that's left of you – a voice
Intangible and deaf
But I will not relinquish you
As even now I strain my hearing
When you finally finish dying
Then I'll strain my memory

The soldier answers him – however
How quickly you have moved
Me down into the roadside darkness
The ditch-side feather grass

So I am bodiless so why
Are you already moving on?
I ask you know not that you cry
I simply ask that you slow down

I'm now a voice – you be a voice
And then we'll flow together
Soon you'll continue down your path
And I'll remain as water
To lie in the earth's oarlock

The soldier counters him: through me
You'll not continue farewell
It's not for us to rive the course of things
But for the Secret One Who is more firm
Than we in definitions – so farewell

What is this? A grey zeppelin passing through red clouds.
Who is this? A pale gentleman without a hat or glasses.
He stands on the embankment, looking at the sunset.
He walks along it, fiddles with his sleeve.

Then he descends. There's sand. Remains of fish and birds.
The east no longer sends him piercing sheets of lightning.
This only: to the west a bit, first red, then blue,
Elusory as mercury, there's still the inclined
Glow of the night skies, night valley-depths,
And through it, like a fattened demon, speeds the zeppelin.

Piercing the bottoms of light clouds,
Once in a while it casts a beam
Onto the crests of preying waves,
Scratching a bit, at the same time,
The seafloor, and the flaneur's face ;
As a bull headed for the slaughter,
It plods in darkness and through darkness,
Illuminating aimlessly how
A certain someone down below
Removes his slippers one by one and
In drunkenness / oblivion,
Embraced / eaten away by sorrow,
Enters the water, starts to plod.

Going as long as the beam guides him,
Through cold, the silence of the waters,
And through the transitory fear.
He walks, as if there were somewhere.
Before him – water, beneath – water,
He timorously breathes out *yes*,
And circles, circles in the waves.

Vrubel's Swan Princess, hung up by her wings,
Is suffocating on a hanger in my wardrobe.
Like willow leaves, her feathers fall onto the shore.
Aren't you my cooling star?
Aren't I your astronomer?

Isn't it I who look at you as you bleed whiteness?
Your hem's embroidered in white corpuscles.
Your neck's embroidered in black corpuscles.
I look and look at you – my star Swan. Later – I say to everyone.
Everything later. Right now I'm looking at my star Swan.
At how she rustles-disappears.

Not in a gilded cage.
But in my stinking wardrobe.
Not in a crystal coffin –
In my stinking wardrobe.
Awaiting eagerly that date, when I shall merge with her.
As if awaiting eagerly a Minotaur, a Unicorn, that mischief-maker Madame
        de Merteuil.

In my wardrobe … What's the matter?
Ku-ku!
Don't lose heart! Our end's behind us.
Before us lies the hour of the swaying lights.
Bushes of fireworks of a Michurin splendor
Will spill – on black, on lilac
(As Blok loved).
And we'll throw back our head and say:
O YES!

But the Groom will look into my face
Say
Forget about him
        Forget about them
                Forget about her

Forget and forget
And come here and come here

To M. L. Lozinskii – with gratitude

O king of forests!
Do not pour the leperous distilment
                              into the porches of the ears.
Do not steal, with hebona in a vial,
Upon the sleeping king of gardens.

O king of marshes!
Spare him. Spare his living blood:

The poison with a sudden vigor turns
The blood – like
              acid dropped in milk....

Now you're as helpless as the elder Hamlet
And I'm as groundless as the younger Hamlet

Meanwhile, the pearly hollow of the ear
Turns white among the agate-colored ringlets.

Recalling for me vividly the incident with uncle.

Let me, with my tongue soaked in leprosy,
Enter your middle – closer to the brain.
Let me enjoy my morning mischief,
Let me observe how pain impales
A handful of dreams.

Now the ghostly imperial ermine
Shakes soapy spray off from its fur,
Now, like a rounded piece of soap, it slips out, melts...

As foul scabs plastered all of Lazarus's
Body with an instant crust,
So my tongue, so my vial of hebona
Plastered you, dear mollusk, and made you me.

A CHRISTMAS PHYSIOLOGICAL SKETCH

M. G.

If the Christmas tree's alive
Like my momma said,
Why is there a knife wound
Gaping in its side –
In its only leg?

      A wound just like that cripple has,
      Who beats his cane against the druggist's window,
      And gabbles in a tongue that never was. . . .

He's swaddled in all sorts of cloth,
A firebird shows off upon his skirt;
And from his every side stick out
(as from a busted, let's say, telephone)
Pieces of wire and of rubber tubing.

      They yell at him, that on the count of Christmas
      The nasty druggist has closed up his shop
      And in a rage the cripple bellows,
      And hoots, and cries out, like an owl.

Under the skirts, his leg discharges puss.
Like the tree's trunk, and resin drips.
But he strides proudly, like a queen.
The California foliage rustles
Under his crutch, and the horizon steams.

Another impression of Prague

Not too far from the place where Doctor Kafka is at rest,
Where one could fathom souvenirs, tourists, a press,
There's emptiness, a shop beset with emerald ivy-tresses.
I'll sit a little while and go.
Left right directly straight-ahead.
A worn-out cross, a wretched cat, a pit.
Lieutenant So-and-so, Averchenko, and next to him – the mother
Of one of our favorite (mine and yours)
Thought humidifiers, enshrouders
Of the *dull* truth about life (which they say is like pus),
Lies here at the edge of Prague. Alone, poor thing.
Above her is a grave – a slouch and scatterbrain,
Above her, scratching its belly, sits a mongrel,
And from afar Prague bellows with mysterious babel.
She lies here at the edge of Prague, beneath wet needles.
It is so dark and quiet. I believe Daphnis and Chloe
Would without hindrance here surrender to their joys
Atop a resin-perfumed carpet, alive and rusty.
On the outskirts of Prague lies his mother, the one who
Washed him in a basin, pouring water from a pitcher and singing.
And it seemed to him that all of her – was like a tower,
The body of a giantess soared, billowed, faded out
Into the darkness, while he was just a gob, a wad, a lump
Beneath her hand – a gob, a wad, a lump.
Her hand emitted warmth, the smell of home,
Up to that time when nowhere smelled of home
To him. But even this warmth and charm,
And her transparency, uneasiness, and burr,
Like any form of love, proved, finally, a real bore,
Nothing was left.
She died alone – he could not come,

Regarding such an impulse – as an impulse, as a whim.
And he stayed where he sat: at the table, *in his little glasses,*
The cat dug glumly through the pieces left to it,
The bird stared straight ahead with its round, lifeless eye,
And they told him that in Prague his mother died.
Sorrow sorrow and sorrow – he lies nude upon white,
And she laughs at her height, like a tower,
And with her pearly body and her stellar body and her snowy body
Shields him from the word *odd* and the word *horrid.*

CHOPIN

I. P.

Like Hecate's knot, he goes to pieces,
Gnawed by a calculating rat.
He pours across the flesh of Dionysus
Like the dead fingernails of purple grapes.

Rain dying down, like a child's bleating,
Buried in warmth and pompously sniffling.
Rain dying down, like a moist meeting:
Iron of springs trembling and sniveling.

Rain, filling up the shadow of bleak memory's
Mariana Trench, bloodless and endless.
My rain, stolen by me and stealing me.
Rain of the rotten, fresh Petersburg suburbs.

Go to the bakery, turn at the market
The infant listens like a new-caught fish,
Opens his mouth just like a triangle,
And spits up thinly, winking mockingly.
It doesn't hurt? No. Now it doesn't hurt.
Gorzovskii plays the piano soothingly.

The infant listens, head inclined,
Drooling and looking over here.
The rain dies down. Danaë writhes.
From pleasure, or perhaps – from shame.

NEW POEMS

(2005–2009)

My every interlocutor
Keep silent scare or pray
Remains so far away
No one will turn to me

Is it my language that's to blame
Or is it my peculiar way
Of life I cannot claim
A fellow tightrope-walker.

Below: both pugs and elephants,
Thawed bald spots like big boulders
And harlequins' pajamas.
Above: the most unpleasant light
Of a projector, a parade of planets.
The orchestra pit's hiss
And broken speech are all around.

My fabled friend,
See how it's all so simple:
To glide by on the smoothness of the dark,
To make out the canals and bridges,
And circumnavigate the towers
Of the guards – so simple.

I'll teach you everything:
To glide along – to gird like me.
And if you'd like – both woe and wit,
And if you'd like – chiaroscuro.
Make sure that you don't fall behind,
But whistle, grimace, sing on high:

Parum-parum off to the sky
Dum-dum to rack and ruin.

Ravaged brothers ravaged
Is this heart of mine.
I am sprouting cabbage
In this heart of mine.
And parsley that is tart,
Parsnips that are sweet.
Don't cry, little Punch doll –
No one is at fault.

Here, a lemur wags his elbows
Shakes his shoulders,
Runs up the branches jostling his hips.
He's a ringer for Nijinsky with his childlike face.
Shamed and abashed, he glances at your father's face.

Your father, who holds by the hand
Something sharp and magical
He no longer knows its name
But he feels its warmth
(Indifferent, enormous, waning)
He looks up and reads on the clouds
Like the count on a baseball scoreboard
In a stadium: "She's so much.
The day was. Not me."

You are foreshortened tortured hemmed
As with the fur spoiled by the father's senselessness.

To me
He seems a whale, which hides amid the depths
From motley babbling fish.
In his motion – slowed and lengthened –

There's something of the motion of stones
In the seething bright-black waters of March
Beneath the windows of the Philosophy Department (Pliny, spleen).
Your father is weightless and mighty –
The timorous Latin
Of the eternally rushing-off psychiatrist
No, it will not catch up with him.

Your father now holds Frosya by the hand. The hand –
Should be memory's last stop
Before it swims off into the abyss.
The palm wraps round the night trains of remembrance,
Proust's soggy little madeleines,
And VN's Dobuzhinskii caves.
And Frosya's wooly head
Is pressed against the tender web of veins,
Stretched out across the father's ruin
Like a sweet lover's furrow.

The hand. To hand. He walks into the room, where I sit without light,
As if I'm Heracles, ensnared with Admetus,
Hoping to save someone, yet lingering.
And mumbles: "I'm still. How cold. Give me that."
And grasps my hand in a despairing handful,
The sweaty palm – awakened, warmed,
Blooms, nearly, like a stump on a spring day,

What's astonishing – your father doesn't know
Who I am, in that room looking after him,
Judging about him,
Yes, and in general, himself. Druid and asteroid,
He moves in darkness,
He moves towards me,
So as to freeze above me, and for a long time warm my hands
In the comfortless silence of his haggard rooms.

Since he has long ago forgotten all our names,
Let him give names to us: Madness and Death.

It substitutes me for myself.
My scent, my tongue, my day.
Like the sheet spread over the dead.
Fear substitutes sloth, gluttony, and lust for me.
It clings to me! It clings, it clings.
Transparent, thin, delicate mushroom
Soaked through with bewitched poison –

I hear this poison everywhere.
G-d be with him you say G-d be with him.
Back I laugh back at you.
I knew no fear then
When I appeared before you.

During the flood – the water
The dull and steady knocking of the logs
The pavement – everything swims up and off like hot air balloons.
More obdurate than tetter, blazing heat,
And steadier than night –
My fear of returning to that estate
Where I stand over you.
We have wind there, contours of bodies,
We have wind there – and chalk.
I pet your head,
Caress the emptiness.

My fear was always on my track,
My fear had led me there and back.

Why do I go
Again up to the open window –

It's lively there: water and fires.
Nestle up to the heavenly fire.
Slumber, slumber.

MADENESS (URBAN TABLEAUX)

(with *Pavel Filonov, Evdokiia Glebova, Tatiana Glebova, and Sayat-Nova*)

Explanatory Preface

The wife of the painter Ph was likely very light
And likely it was this that let him
Carry her through the entire city
In his arms when she had fallen
In a faint at a tram stop
On the way to the Kresty Prison to meet her two sons –
Peter and Aleksei.

He was told that she was at the hospital
He hurried there and carried her right out
Throughout this pausing for a breath just once
On the bridge across the Karpovka River.
And thus he ran across the city with Ekaterina Semenovna in his arms.
She after all was very light: due to her age –
Twenty years older than the painter Ph.

"Twenty years older! Twenty years older!"
"He called her Daughter, didn't use her name! He called her Daughter, didn't
        use her name!"
Exclaims perplexedly the painter's sister – in her careful,
Somewhat simple-hearted reminiscences.

Monolog of the Painter Ph on the Bridge Across Karpovka

Daughter.

My baby-child is wearied suffered plenty
And calmly sleeps while faithful Painka-Pan'ka

Has tidied up the room sits reads and works
Daughter will get everything Panka's promised.
Compared to you I look like a wax doll, clumsily made.

Goodnight daughter Ekaterina – Semenovna
Your little grey legs sleep like tired little ducks in winter grass.
It's raining.
Your Panka, your Painka loves the rain.
This meager music.

There's no such mysticisim
There is no such trash
In my creations.

View from the Top

Darling Ekaterina Semenovna!
Pity your legs have given out!
And you don't mount the roof with me
And you cannot do not look out with me
Black burning sky above the icy river.

An inflammation of bombers
An eruption of anti-aircraft guns
The hump of Isaac's Cathedral
The Admiralty's withered thread

Pity that you've not
Legs to follow him
That which is open to the gaze upon the roof
Is sharper
Than a dream.

The city – oh my daughter –

Has pressed itself to me with a dead scream
And chirps, and whispers, and oinks – like an exploding shell.
You, my Panechka, do not avert your gaze
From the paralytic waters of the Karpovka River beneath the rainbow-
    colored snow
From the lovely slackened bodies, locked into cubes of ice.

....

....

On the corner of Stremiannaia and Marata streets I saw one.
On the corner of Stremiannaia and Marata streets I saw one.

With a face that was blindingly clear, and a dress that was blindingly green.
I looked at her and I did not go blind. I looked at her and looked.
(as it befits those in love,
seized by desire – to look)

Ekaterina Semenovna, death retreats beneath the pressure of the gaze.
I looked at her through festive rainbow-colored ice.
And I did not go blind, I waited – soon my turn will come.

Either the roof shakes me off with the wind's blinding touch,
Or gives me the slip with a shell,
Or I will be stifled
And expire and be left here to stand
Like a cube made of ice
Like a pillar of salt
Like a daughter of Sodom
And to look from the height of a smallish brick house
As cubes of ice burn everywhere in blackness.

A Stroll

Daughter Ekaterina Semenovna,
Be kind to me, now, for the sake of G-d

Hand, take the golden seal!

With my darling I'll stroll through the Summer Garden
There at the gate There at the fence
Chronos, time's G-d,
Lays his soft-boned children
On his tooth
And smack and pop and plop

I am your servant – lend me vision.
For you I will take everything.
Lend me vision from above, give me a name –
That windy, fractious, changing name of yours.

Not to be grasped – it scampers off – like steam, like bugs, the
      undergarments
Of the Queen of Spades – the two-faced duchess,
Stripping before Hermann – ah, I'm a naughty girl,
I've squandered everything.
I've lost the *silver cigarette* case!
From now on
I won't look at you, my rueful dandy-killer.

Ekaterina Semenovna
Covers her aged face –
   Let us go strolling, Panechka, past the gutter-canals.
   I will unveil the city's every wrinkle.

Epilogue – Dialogue

Glebova – First

Yes, I am his sister
In the sense

That I read his thoughts
From evening until morn.

I come I watch he hides behind the drawing board
In his face, so alertly-erased,
Attention and coldness,
And his eyes never once rested.

He never rested,
Read many journals.
It may be that he never died,
When he would tear off airy fragments
For his wife.
He said all the while – "why for me, better – for daughter"

Glebova – Second

Yes I am your sister
In the sense
That I read your thoughts
From evening until morn.
But I outlived you
On the seventh of December.

I rose I washed I went to fetch the water
On the way I met his sister.
He died. If they can get a coffin they will bury him.
Almost the whole town is submerged in darkness.
He died.
And if they cannot get a coffin – they won't bury him.

His marvels glint off the walls like pearls – surely they move.
While he himself lies on the table draped in white
With white binding his head.

Thin as a mummy.
His eyes have sunk. His eyes rest.

By his side only Ekaterina Alexandrovna,
Paralyzed, tongueless, helpless woman.
His sisters too are old and helpless.

Glebova – First

Yes I am his sister
Saved him
For seven days buried his body
Awaited destiny, a date.
Then carried, carted,
Wanted.

I come I watch after his memory
A tongueless sister – I think him.

Glebova – Second

Yes I am his sister
I am his student
He's reached his end
And I hold him within me.

His lifelong absence was for me
A sign – fine: work, send word.

I visit him for tea
I bring him a small circle of an onion, cube of soap

On Serafimovskoe Cemetery
I visit him.
I'm 90.
I tell him: look, today the light,
Like dirty water, is uneven – it freezes, flows.

He's angered now – I was so sure about you!
Look more attentively!

Epilogue - Monologue

What has this to do with you?
Do with me? Why, not a thing.
Panechak, now, have you truly
Stuck your shoulder in the paint;

Now here's a shoulder that is blue
Now here's a shoulder that is white
Glinting in the darkness palely,
Shimmering with heat.

Panechka, more, more –

For me your city's death.
For me it's now unsealed.

G-d will not betray.
G-d will not betray.
The swine won't eat the infant.

I. Blue Lights and Flares over the Shallows

Turner's engaged in tournament
.... With Constable, with the Academy,
.... With fine weather, with foul weather,

An ill-starred melee
With a stain of green,
Which battles like a harried ship –
O teeth of cliffs,
O swirls of black.

.... He's gloomy, he is silent,
.... He gnaws a herring filthily.

Turner detests the hoopskirt
Of his mousy mistress
At any minute, god forbid, she'll spark a migraine
Poor man he roars
He searches for his cane.
Finds it and wanders off

To where the sea's above,
To where the sand is pierced all over –
Like a noble chief
Of some sea-faring tribe –
With shattered seashells,

And out of them stick tufts of sea grass
As from the armpits of a dead old woman.

He touches with his cane.
He drafts upon the sand:

Now here's the ship,
Now here, rising above it,
Lengthening, a cloud,
Huge as a newborn's
Mouth upon a teat,

Now here...

The farewell tenor of the empty wind
Cries out for Turner (why does it scream so?)
Now he has spit unto the sand,
Now Turner has looked back –

Darkness approaches him,
So as to see the sunset:
The fire's green shrub
And the bay's blond bite,
And Turner backs away, not so much gutlessly, –
Abashedly, and hurries –
Off from the sea, and off from me.

II. Trade

The goddess of the sea gave me,
To me the goddess of the sea gave
Three shells that ripened at the bottom,
That brought fruits to the bay's slim brim,
Fruits of abysses and of rainbow silt.

The goddess of the sea has wrapped about me
A wave's fierce hand, squeezed and licked off

The silver earrings from my ears,
That quick and supple is her sting!

And the gray rings descended to the bottom –
Into the spacious jewelry cases
Of the chesty, herring-like
Maidens,
Doomed to their desert dreams,
As seashells that are ripped up from the bottom.

One will be found among them:
Fishlike, a March sea cuke, an evil fishy:

She swims and iterates into the shell,
And in response the shell fumes out this tune:

I am used to being lonely,
As a seashell at the bottom,
Light blue silence would dissolve
Into bubbles and rise up.
In the dark and in the deep
'Neath the wave, above the wave
Silent light streams 'cross the bottom,
As in a serene-blue dream.
In this silence so abhorrent
In this silence so aberrant
I live down upon this blackened
And this very distant bottom

Wear, then, the earrings – let them blacken
Upon your ears, which are so nervous, sensitive,
Let swarms of fish, like circus lions through a hoop,
Jump melancholically through them.

They will protect you
From idleness, from anger, and from longing,
As not a single haughty
Groom could do.

Wear them – rejoice – my mermaid – glimmer,
As an evil glint, across the water, of another shore's reflection,
Be evil silver, an abyss, be motion,
Be evil silver of the unseen swarms of fish.

Homeless man sleeping near the Charles
What are your dreams – measured? Or mild?
How gaily monotone the paddling
Of the augustly swimming galleys
Of Harvard's team. "Row on! Row on!"
Their coach, that bull, whoops through his horn.

You, near the wave, like a wet parrot
Have calmed – chimeras vex your mind,
But cautiously: a smile's steam spills
Across your lips, so that rogue Tristan
Had once lain, fragrant and fetid.
The fog dripped juice – swelling the dawn.
And stillness, like a linen cloth
Shamedly draped the waters' wound.

Tristan could sense and know his fate,
So much like you – helpless he lay,
Having outfoxed himself, but not the fox-
Death, which pleads ("soft…") for you to come.
And smack – there's no way out.
Crawl, fly, or draw
A frightened mark in place of your own name.

Without a name, a body, or a face,
But with a blanket, with a heel, and with a beard –
You lie above the varicolored water.
White-handed Isolde, upon noticing the stranger,
Shrieks so sharply, and the bright tone of her face
Blends with the boiling foliage
And is transfigured.

Here sits a madman. Why's he sitting?
Is he virtuosically angry at me,
Or do I take the place of another?
He bums my cigarettes, he stinks,
He winds to a gavotte-like beat.
What I vaguely imagine to be a gavotte –
Something slow, something sort of like that.
But since I've got nothing to do, here I am
Watching a crazy man, standing,
Next to the hotel. Someone will soon arrive
In a beautiful green car.
Again he'll be late by an hour or so
For supposedly mysterious reasons,
And his accent (as well as his kiss)
Will be soft, and pleasant to the taste.
As I finally climb into his car,
He hands me an apple. "Blow,"
He says, "off the European road dust,
The smoke of Goethe's and So's homeland. "
The foreigner reads me between the lines.
That is why it's so easy for me.
There was a time, another gray-haired joker
On payday would bring home
These very apples, but to remember them
I still don't have the strength.
He also listened to me, without changing his expression,
Accompanying me to school, or from,
He also knew beforehand what would happen in the end,
And from outside – what would occur within.
I imparted my verses to him, as to you –
And in this matter, both of you

Are deaf, as you are deaf to my adventures, but
He was jealous and was sorry for me,
Whereas to you – with whom I wander there – it's all the same:
Whoever has me in whatever way,
To you, they're merely peanut shells and puppies.

You wipe from my stiff cheek
A thin coat of rice powder,
Tuck in my blanket just so,
And make sure that darkness would not touch me,
And twist your sagging mouth.

Professor Pnin's little white doggie
A tender gift
A spindle's prick
The little soul flies to the realm of spicy fantasies –
My dream – the little pillow rots with tears!

Timothy the Indomitable
Is released like an arrow
Into the past: beyond the trams
The roof tiles are scarlet.
Turn after Tuchkov Bridge –
The lilac's stench.
The dampish adolescent shame of tenderness,
However, fills your palm.

If I learn to drive a car – I'll take the beauty for a spin.
If I don't learn – the bicycle's dragonfly crackle
Scatters about like iron beads.
Emptiness:coolness.

Emptiness:coolness.
Behind Zhuchka: the granddaughter.
Behind Strelka Point: the Neva.
Behind the right hand – the left hand.

What should I say about life?
Such a tiny little thing,
But so painful and swollen.
Mama, mama, what's your favorite river?

After Tuchkov Bridge, turn – buy meek little wild carnations
Look in on laughing N –
The catwoman, thoughtfully brewing tea.

How idiotic she will say your habits are.
Nevermind you'll say.
Kiss her on the eyes. Farewell.

Anna went to fetch some water,
Found a young man sitting there,
His black beard shaking in the air.

It isn't that he simply sits,
He's not really in a fit,
He laboriously tracks the sunset's blots.

Here, now, with a golden border –
Like a little golden ruble –
Swims a smoky apparition,
Acid-scorched on every side.

Here, enormous as a bee –
The epitome of heat,
A shred of the exhausted sun,
Burned completely, inside out.

After them, hard on their heels –
Black over here, green over there,
Soars a bird right out of Blok, a captain out of Gumilev.

A dark-rusty mugginess,
A crumb of hay, a swarm of midges,
Anna, out of heavy buckets, pours out water on her feet.

Anna comprehends the plot,
Gnaws a reddish strand of hair,
A reddish beam on a reddish neck,
Crawling upward like an ant.

Now, already, darkness, like
A red stream out of the mouth,
Pours from heaven on our faces.
So the bottom line is drawn.

What's the meaning of our meetings –
The river knows, as does the speech,
We're to recollect and not,
And to guard our ignorance.

I.

Approaching the Polish village of O in a van.
I shock myself – why don't I feel a thing.

As if my soul's a lacerated senseless gum,
A dentist's entertainment, Rodenbach's city of slumber.
The main thing is to move like canal water – that is, not move. If you but
      budge your arm – mad shadows barge into your calm.

All of these Rosas, Ludwigs, numbered for us,
So that we count them over as the gas is loosed.

We counted, by the way, through indirect signs: pots, dentures, glasses,
Red-lined, black-lined magic little shoes,

Suitcases, hairs, ash, sagging clouds,
A student's hand turned purple from the cold
Digs into an umbrella. Cuckoo
Of Birkenau – tell me, how many futher years
Need I pay visits to these moralizing barracks?
Cold cold hot:
The blindman's bluff of civilized awareness.

I don't feel anything but shame
At flicking ashes from a Marlboro
On ashes made here, poured out here.

II.

This little stone here is a monument to him.
This cloud here is a butt, a buttercup, a dog –
All that he couldn't take with him into the gloom,
Though till the last he didn't gripe but lugged.

This tree here is a john, a bench, a poppy –
All of the horror's trash, of shit's despair,
I, garish and self-satisfied magician,
Bring you – skip off and see the movie

Of things that play as in a dream:
A crushed pince-nez winks,
A saucepan grunts, an alarm clock rules the night,
A chewed up pencil-stub scribbles:
Our master, our provider, our caretaker,
We would so gladly help you
 – don't know how.
This little stone here is your final mark.
Non-exclamation. Splinter. Umbrella. Grain.

On Monday
I enter my office
Discover:
A bird
Tried to reach me.
It left on the window
A silhouette, an imprint,
A pinch of shit.
A biography's not-too-dry sediment.
A stir
Of feathers dropped in the hurry of perishing.

But if this proves too little for the fastidious researcher,
We'll press our face against the glass,
Look down.
This is where she fell,
This is how someone sucked and gnawed at her.
That is when, under the sway of the night's dews, she turned
Lighter than sand, more definite than metal.

(are you serious? You're serious about all this?
Zero empathy, a pinch of curiosity)

A colleague
A professor of art history
Enters the office to bum a smoke.
Well, that's certainly something – she says – By the way, this is exactly how
        Poussin conceives of Lethe.
Transparent flatness.
On its reverse side – for us – is everything for which there are no words,
        which means, there's no commiseration.

There is one's suffering at the inadequacy of the means of description,
There's the temptation
Of an appeal to melo-
Declaration – "here you lie, delicate piece of chalk,
Not long ago you sang you laughed you sang,
And were so pleasant to our organs of sensation."

And now: not this, nor that, not the body, but an impression of the body
Etched with a dry needle on the plate of vision.
The pain of others (Montesquieu whispered) everyone bears.
Meanwhile, behind the glass someone burns up with darkness,
As with, let's say, envy or thirst.

The Muse of History awakes on January 1st
With eyes full of pus.

Without saying a word to herself, weakly moaning,
She heads for the mirror:
The spectacle is harsher –
The right eyelid won't lift: Salute to Vii!
The left is the pink-blue of a white night at daybreak.
Like the enticing micas
Of Bazhov's tales,
The world is refracted, meager and unsightly,
Into a foggy, intermittent glimmer.

The New Year, through such optics,
Looks like a shelled-out building:
In a room torn up by the explosion
A calendar is hanging on the wall: onward, climber!
What onward could that be – rhetorically it's obviously up,
But the wall tries down…

The glued lid is so warm, it makes one sick.
Clio, grown cockeyed, squats and starts to creep:
Because for History there is no stop.

Her movement is dangerous, especially because
it wishes to seem meaningful to the observer:
In actuality,
a giant Gull
Has clutched you to her stomach,
And you dissolve into her helpless body.

Like that wag Griboedov, the crowd determines you're an idler,
Tears off your paws, mustaches, wings, and squeezes out a drop of juice:
You become – a squeezed-out vine, grain broken by the flail, a greasy petal's
       lace:

A petal that is shaggy, purple:
In Berkeley, Shattuck intersects with Ward:
I used to live here teach you to observe-deceive.
And now, an anonymous faceless succeeding one lives here:
He won't check on my acorn! won't water mama's poppy!

History you are indignant History
Memory you are surprised Memory

The victor struts into the city
The city is alive and dead
How I need how dear to me
Is the tempter of the cities
The redeemer of the cities

Shaven-headed he is awful
Height-wise he is not so grand
But to tyrants of black towers
And to tyrants of red towers
He sticks out his tongue

His tongue is sprung
His tongue's boom-boom
Arrayed swear-swear
Not unlike a tongue of flame it runs across the curls of girls
Across birches, across branches

The victor is all wounds
All open like a screen
Let me sprinkle on the wounds
Let me drink from them

Victor-and-dismemberer
Sets out for the city-din
Determiner of hidden forms
Sets out for the city-mind

He left his granny and he left his grandpa
He fled from the KGB
He fled across the Finnish ice

He stomached the Aurora Borealis in his mighty gut
He was unloved in Berlin
Unsociable in Petersburg
Guarded in Moscow by a certain someone

I want to be with him!

The victor struts into the city.

I.

AngelAnna leans over a homeless madman
Who has installed himself atop a manhole cover.
The November night's demons finger the bows,
As they would phalluses, as they would lyres.
Sonorous-arrows will now fill up with an icy seed
So as to pierce the hapless fellow.
Anna strokes the reeking man as if he were a shifty, panting mongrel.

The squeamish residents of Philadelphia slip by above us.
The demons of the night have hid behind the lights.
Let's go, Anna, let's go – we're in a hurry – and he is fine here anyway –
In the warm vomit on the black lace of the manhole cover.
His shirt fluffs up like hauberk with his frozen sweat.
Let's go, Anna, the demons of the night no longer scare him.

II.

AngelAnna looks at another AngelAnna.
In San Francisco, on a sunny day, she looks, committing her to memory.
What else can one do with an angel,
Absorb it with the eye,
Subdue it with the steely feathers of the eyelash,
While a burst vessel sprays across the eye the blood of the observation's
        intensity.

She looks, committing her to memory,
As the burgeoning, breaking, coastal line
Of the cheekbone climbs up –

To the very top.
There lie demolished towers,
The yellow boiling of the ocean.

Such are the pleasures of angels:
To embalm with a gaze.
To lock up in the memory as in a room.
On the wall – a reproduction of a Desiderio.
On the table – a reproduction of a Desiderio and a chewed stub.

There, a demolished tower. There, an atrocious surf slurps.
There in the sand are sullied hair your hands.
There a jellyfish lies on the sand like a friendly small eye.

III.

AngelAnna awakes in the morning announces her dream's synopsis: "I – am
    a bone"
What do you mean what do you mean I assure her you – are a guest
The messenger of PseudoDionisius Areopagite
The affirmation of the apophatic view of G-d
The negating particle un
The form of love that doesn't lend itself to words:
Fi-un-cée
Un-touchable
Un-conductive
Across the places of an inflamed childhood,
Strewn with trampled glass.
Without enticement – charm.
Without penetration – reflection
In the densely populated ribbon of the tide.

Pacific Ocean. Five o'clock in the evening. Winter.
For the purpose of acquaintance and possible caresses

Frosya
decisively advances on a dog.
The half-dachshund fearfully
glances at the waves. The winter sun is vapid as a persimmon
Dissolved by the horizon's acid.
The half-dachshund appeals in thought to his mistresses: "at the moment of
      danger – where are you?"
They chatter smoke shake sand out of their shoes.
But now, they're in a hurry – half-angels-half-maidens.
Frosya is disenchanted the Dachshund snitches
The roar of the waves muffles the traitorous voice

IV.

AngelAnna formulates her question: why do the clouds flutter?
Do they flutter? Rather, they move!
Not so: they flutter like seaweed in water at night,
Like the bodies of sleepers.
Watching over the sleepers – are angels.
But the sleepers themselves – are angels.

Here they lie in the dark like shimmering pieces of ice.
Detached from the flow of the night by their harsh destination.
Huge sleeping icy carcasses flutter in the crowded winter sky.

V.

A fox jumps cross the snow.
Throughout New England, forests
Are glued packed up with snow
Here is a homophone of sky:
Reyneke Forest is as sharp as a scarlet devil
And is engaged in the same sort of lustrous running.

Like two columns in a diary
All is divided here:
Good and Evil.
The fox is red, and all is white.
And at this point everything –
AngelAnna notices with a smile –
That winter's issued to the view is warm.
Warmth – my faulty chaperon and fetish.
The fox, run off a bit, sees all – observes:
My reeking burning thimbleful of heat.

Like a delicate, humorous word in a vacuum
Like a furtive forgiving and curious gaze
Like the smell-taste of childhood not saccharine but sweet –

Is the fox's jump-flight on a primered canvas.

VI. The Parting of Angels

One AngelAnna forgets the language of the other.
The signifier does not match the signified: as in a game
No effort clarifies – what the word meant:
Illness? An animal? The wind's direction?
An empty sound is left, a purpose-driven dash.

The Angel thrusts out words like things while moving.
And let's the other Angel have a look at them: maybe they still suffice?
But no, they just won't do at all: they're full of mildew, hatred, adulation.
Discard him – I don't want him.

The Angels dim, but still glance at each other dumbly:
Out of their mouths fly rainbow bubbles.

The matter isn't inability, but numbness.
We come undone, we part ways: one-two-three.

Bitter proud thick as late-Baroque allegories
Possessors of a host of inexpressible meanings
They part like duelists who have lost their living minds,
Having forgotten to turn round and take a shot –
Having forgotten, grown distracted in the search for words: angels – these
        are the ones that…
Into oblivion's gray gluey mass the last word will be lost – the word
        "furiously"

Thunderstorms happen over Poland

From a morning table talk

I.

I'm standing on the outskirts of a castle, which served varieties of -ists,
Masters in ironed uniforms. A hawk glides by below.
At panorama's edge in oily air.
Should I now drop a tear:
Why am I not a hawk and do not fly
Why am I not a falconer and do not try
The hawk with a silk leash?

My task is strict: I'm hiding, I observe
How he commingles with the sky. The hawk will not
Drop tears for anyone:
Only for prey –
For a tender-skinned bittern,
For a redolent fox,
For a blubbery marmot.

Hawk-angel, you have thrown a quiver over shoulders overgrown with
        feathers.
Do you still dangle on a line
For the castle's masters who so love the panorama
Or are you now already just a bit of what you really are?
Is Poland still your pretty cockeyed courtesan
Or is there other news?

Hawk, you stand above it all:
You see small pieces –

See the rivers' twists, the stunts of flattened streets,
Here, are eight-year-old girlfriends
Looking with reproof
At a puppy that's suddenly fallen asleep in the sun,
Here, is a nun that speeds to make the train,
Here, is an infant that's awoken – his cheek –
A lithographic print of mama's blouse. A tale
Of itty-bitty and unspeakable events. St. Francis
Tries to get something across to an embittered snail.

The hawk, noticing this, throws himself downward:
At the pied tiles
Of fields, of gardens, parking lots – he's agitated
By his work as warden
By his unbounded knowledge.

Ringing breaks out of St. Ann's Church,
The pilgrims – as if storming a fortress – climb up the hill –
Too late, – the hawk is touched – too late.

From the imaginings of Konstanty Ildefons Gałczyński

R.R.

II.

"Enchanted horse
Enchanted coach
Enchanted coachman."

The final match
Will light the rider's face
A telegram clasped tightly in his hand
The final ma... – the hand is licked
By little tongues of flame.

Along the other hand a girl's affixed herself
Skinny and black – an ancient shaft.
Yes, the banner was burned long ago.
The rider doesn't even notice his companion:

"Will Artur and Ronard really not come
For him out of the lanes, whose wash-house chatter
Is more sour than the taste of wine at midnight.

Enchanted coachman,
Enchanted horse,
Enchanted coach.

A midnight square
And florid dreams of signs:
BUTCHER and BARBER
BUTCHER and PRIEST

BUTCHER and BUTCHER
DRAFTSMAN OF MONEY
OTHELLO and TAXIDERMIST

In Kraków's Old Town Square it's circle after circle
In Kraków's Old Town Square it's one after another

And air imbued with beer and onions
As the coach crawls onto the bridge.

So what does the rider chatter, awaking,
You, Mashenka, are jealousy and prettiness and ovary,
Across the Vistula-flowing-death.

The butcher cleaves the burning udder.
What is the matter with my hands,
And something's doubling with my letters
And in my hand the telegram
Is melting darkening: Enchanted horse
Enchanted coach
Across a black square and a red square
The tram gains speed

It's overtaken by the coachman Ben Ali.

Look in the gap between the houses blazes
The vanished Kraków Snow
The vanished carrier the vanished airier
And in the beer a ginger syrup
And Kraków's long wandering nights
The vanished roughhewn sketch.

From the Podgórski Market Square to Lwowska Street
The oblivion of Jewish glory blazes
Smoke roiling in the March air melts –
Ben Ali watches

He repeats –
What else did you see?

From the Podgórski Market Square – I saw beds and chairs
Suitcases, nooses. So from a dead hive
Like buzz – a sweet stink flies.
Ben Ali watches

As the rider bends, clasps the telegram,
Repeats:
ENCHANTED SQUARE
ENCHANTED COACH

And of a sudden – weeping, yelling, croaking:
"Empty will be –
Empty will be –
My sweetest Kraków."

My mother burned herself with poisonous ivy, and Frosya washes her
hand.

As Thumbelina fallen in the clutches of the mole
Or the mole snared in Thumbelina's sticky fingers –
What am I carrying on about? – meaning – what am I weaving?
Is it really a secret pattern from a senseless wire?
Whom do I listen to? – meaning – whom do I blame?

Poisonous grass drills through a vacant summer.
Now just like plastic you flow closer to the fire –
You'll sprout sores, sprout blisters, all for fun.
Nearer the fire of pities that hang in the heat.
You go, as if cutting through honey, and remember, and know
That you don't remember anything at all, don't know
And write about this to the neighbor the tailor's sister:

"For a week now our plastic heat is poisoned.
The little one sits by the stream, which hiccups, grows shallow.
While I sense on my ample, inflamed back
A shirt that might as well have been constructed by Medea.

The little one digs with a yellow holey bucket –
Thumbelina is a small sublingual ball of coolness.
While I sense thunderstorms amassed beyond the bridge,
And, as if delirious, a tired grasshopper repeats,

That all this isn't about that. Or is it about that?
That thunderstorms and tonsils fill with grass's poison,
That you adjust your yellow holey kerchief,
My sublingual chill, forever by my side."

My chill, my blowing, my revelation of the wind, my nod,
Here is the dimple here – as if crossed with a tress

The foot and the leg, goose-grass, the shoulder and the stomach.
That's all a person gives, prepared for an embrace.

Teensy-weensy, delicate, and nervous, with a kerchief and bucket.
With a haughty pock-mark in a smile weary of heat.
The thunder opens idly, like an old umbrella,
The palms, like swollen kidneys, are bright and claggy.

An empty chatty idle dour day
Crawled to the sea floor. With a booming howl
The monstrous wolves wake witches,
Who will entice the night,
Which sprays upon us pus and tragic sorrow,
Which with its slow and sleepy wings, as if with keys,
Knows how to open graves.
The graves' unfastened jaws
Reek like a quarantine for cholera, like ruddy silt.

What do you feel yourself to be on nights like this?
A pimple on the brow of angered Hecate,
Whose menstrual blood distends the sunsets
Across the surface of the skies?

A purposeless and hopeless pawn
Running along a toad-stool lane
Through Propp's unfriendly forest?

Where is your friend defender? What's to help?
All is unknown tomorrow, lies, anxiety,
Your stomach turns, things glint before your eyes,
A Dantesque panther lies upon a branch
And smirks – all of a sudden sulfur boils,
"Give me a lick," – whispers the cyanide.

Everything's foreign. Foreign sky. The depths.
My gurgling consciousness, like a dried peel,
Is pressed out by a foreign speech.
My angel slathers lavishly onto stale bread
All that I do not need.

Only with sugar, pressed in the small handle
Of a two-year-old beauty's rattle
Will a mysterious word flash before me –
Don't be afraid of them. They are but shades, but shades.
Fines for a boundless gift for pardoning,
They are but dust the rain will wash away.
And now a person with a rueful smile
Swims into the deliberately-accidental dream.
So as to draw himself out in your name.

The face of love: it is unstable, it is evil.
Its features flame from underneath a layer
Of pride, lust, ignorance, and vanities.
In scars of malady – the mask of Antinous
Rises above the city like the sun.

To LG, OM, STD, and the impatient Cocteau

I'll snatch this story from the depths, by shock tactics. And if fate's against me I'll deal
with fate. I'll cheat it with a card trick. I live in another world, a world where time
and place are wholly mine. I now live without newspapers, letters, telegrams, without
any contact with the outside world at all. The mist lifted this morning but the clouds
crossed, then superimposed themselves one on top of the other, until the whole sky
was covered in layers.
—Jean Cocteau, September 5, 1945, 11 am, notes taken during filming, from *Beauty and
the Beast: Diary of a Film*

1. The Kindness of Strangers Is Such a Thing

It flows down the whiskers seeps into the mouth
It takes you by the soul
Gently not bravely
Like a beginning med student would take a body stiff with cold.

The kindness of strange trees is poor and pale
In Italy, in the church of San Severo
A marble shroud is draped over a marble Him.
Through it the tourists look onto.
the moon

Beneath a strange tree here in Amherst we're distress.
St. Augustine remarked about this kind of space:

You – fields of my memory bestrewn with dried and scentless mignonettes
You – palaces of memory, hung over water
You – caves of memory (who *isn't* here! what *isn't* here!)
Chambers of memory, pockets of memory, match boxes of memory
(these – in difficult times, are closer to dawn)

You – fields of my memory, mottled with pale spruce
Between them
My only friend wanders.

Not animal not bridegroom
Not a pleasant sight

More like: a cloud
Pillar of light
A table covered with a pallid cloth
It's hot on the veranda
Katya sits barefoot
Dima smokes
The dog whips its tail wistfully.
You – field of my memory.

Beneath fierce rain (Hokusai's next reincarnation).

Polina Frosya – we'll wait just a little longer
My mother, freezing, arrogantly scowls

When the light gets bad and the clouds start moving so mysteriously that the assistant cameraman, watching through his orange glass, can no longer see what's going to happen, I lie down on the grass, close my eyes and let my poem (*The Crucifixion*) work on me. It carries me so far away that I lose all contact with my surroundings and, when the look-out man shouts that the sun's coming out again, I must look just as though I am waking from a dream.

—Jean Cocteau, Sunday, 11:30, *Beauty and the Beast: Diary of a Film*

2. The Only Friend

The shadow of me rests upon you
The shadow of you rests upon me

Slowly circling, a cap knocked off a mushroom
Flies to the ground
Ringing a bit
after slight frosts

I recognize you and await and talk to you
Do not agree to anything and fly above you
Fall like a velvet cap screwed off a mushroom
Fall and start writhing all along you

Our pond is dry and frozen from the cold
Oh December: philosophy of absentmindedness tears destitution – our
      Proudhon
The golden pond is cloaked in leaves of suede
Frosya thinks – beneath this gilding-destitution
Her familiar Frog is asleep.

Frosya says: You are my only friend, Froggy!
How goes it?
In a poison-pink jacket
On quickly-melting snow
I sit and ponder you.

You are invisible, but you're so clear to me.
Maybe – you aren't there, but maybe one can't see
You until the spring sets in –
You will arise from the protective bottom.

My only friend – you're good to me in every way.
Just like a faithful shoe you do not squeeze my soul,
Rather caress it
Probably – you are my soul.
But where are you? When will you enter
The shell again?

Or will I be transparent and unfilled,
Amid the whisper and the flutter of the forest
Watch as the weft of rime
And as the warp of a black bush
Create a bitter pattern
A bitter gulp, burning the mucus membrane,
Of life without you.

I'll take Beauty's flight by moonlight. She'll wear her cape and walk the whole length of the house, till she reaches the iron ring decorated with the head of a horned monster. Then she'll look to the right and to the left.
—Jean Cocteau, September 5, 1945, midday, *Beauty and the Beast: Diary of a Film*

3. A Romance About the Moon-Moon: A Nighttime Viewing

The moon isolated by its languor
From dreadful lace stain of the cloud
Crawling forth to devour her.

The bus, in whose corner sits Hitchcock
Pierces the movie like a rusty needle
Full of some narcotic,
As an electric
Current pierces through the hand.

The moon is brimful of its ardor,
Like the cloud which brings me boredom, boredom,
boredom, boredom.

The hero and the author sit on the same bench.
And Cary Grant is frozen on the razor's edge.
A full-fed night moth –
On the pin's thigh
Of the ill fat man who created him.

The moon pours down much like a passenger from an uneasy seat.

The moon is stretched across the heavens like a screen
That same clean sheet of longing, upon which

Hitchcock all huffy
And the spiffy Cary Grant
Are occupied in melancholy.
Melancholy conversation.

What are you doing here – here where – in my moon tarnished in my sweat
in my saliva what are you doing my creator in your own creation –

And what are you doing on my bus –

We both ride grit our teeth live fret about the schedule –

We both gawk at the moon's rim at the black the white frame my boots and
pants squeeze me too tightly while the plot hands you the diamonds
and the dame an azure night so why have you pressed up against me?

As a horse before the rain,
A victim of terrible colic...

And why are you complaining?
I'm a eunuch. (variant: you're a eunuch)
You're a bridegroom. (variant: I'm a bridegroom)

All is a lunar range of senseless calluses.

Pain all night. No sleep. My face is being devoured by some unknown germ, and my
gums eaten into by some other. My face is only a shell of rashes, ravages and itches.
It'll take me all my strength to forget this task, and go on living underneath it.
—Jean Cocteau, September 26, 7 am, *Beauty and the Beast: Diary of a Film*

4. The Soul Is Like a Moon-Shaped Hole

Arranged conveniently for the rolling-swallowing of spheres.
Spheres of anxiety fear thoughts of suicide
(a list of symptoms on the booklet in a box of Prozac)
That take pains to direct themselves into the soul-hole of an iced-up golf
      course.

December.

Look how lilac it is.
Look how silver and lilac it is.
Appreciate how it is etched in ink.

Says a pale woman pining for her homeland
Let's say – in a late novel by I. S. Turgenev

Look: where it is pink below
Where it is gray above
Where it is skin below
Where it is rind above

Our sky: either a decadent or a totalitarian body
With violet traces in place of a sun
Either a vampire's bite
Or the cigarette butt

Of a GPU agent.

Skin-rind.
Is it you – princess – mouse?
Residing in a palace of interwoven branches
A palace of interwoven twilights.
Come to me quick
Before the frenzy of the dark
Come while the colors still transpose themselves, the tones still flutter.
While violet pink lilac purple
Are secreted like saliva
Like Rozanov's wondrous fluids from a beauty's marvelous body.

A play of shadows
on somebody's face
will remind me of you
And I'll feel lighter –
Then darker again.

The film
At the end, when the hero
Has long been killed
Condenses and the captions fall upon the face like rainy pollen
And in the interval between
The flow of credits and the final dialogue
You've hid yourself – and live
Under the name Nobody, like Odysseus.
In the polysemantically-deep pocket of memory.

An octopus hides so upon the seabed
[A simile unfurling like a banner]
He's nervous-pink like fatal flesh,
Many-pimpled and polysyllabic –
Homeric participle.
He's delicate, pink as a baby's mouth
Pressed to its mother,
Mighty as much as paltry,
With mossy and uneven lips,
A magic mouth – a magic cave.

Yes, memory's an octopus.
Devouring and burning us, a living
Medley of nimble feelers
That suddenly crawl up out of the dark.

A million torments ago
We'd briefly been two.
Left, now, is one.
Left, now, without you.
Left, overgrown with other names and times,
Grown with a child
To earth, but that which has become me was once us,
And part of me whines for that state.
Whines pledges bitches
Knows not it's place,
And suddenly explodes and roars with lava,
When I don't know what – say a ghost a voice or gesture
Reminds it of you, calls it down onto the seabed.

And all that follows is gained
In utter uselessness it seems as eh-
Pilogue. And why repeat – here lived the golden flame –
Of her, that sifts through ashes.

The herds plod home
And flocks of birds speed home
And golden shades of fish glide home

There, where all hearts are clear,
Where my love eats, and sleeps, and drinks.
Where my love neither eats, nor sleeps, nor drinks.
He keeps watch: he's the eye of heaven, eye of earth,
He is the eye of day and eye of night.
What is my love?
Is he a heavenly or earthly paradise?

Do you recall the land where lemon bloomed,
Where peaches ripened?
Where there were flowers blue and red?
Where there were red fruit and blue fruit?
Do you recall the circle-rhombus-oval?
Do you see us, inclined over the water?

A fount a lake a stream a river river
Water and wine and blood
Wine water blood
Will leak right through our fingers, through our fingers.
Your hand still touches me
Your love now touches me,
And is like wine and reeds, wine and a spring.

Affectu quem secreto cum cordis amabo,
Nulla pellaris patior detrimenta pudoris;
Ast ubi forte sui merear complexibus uti
Eius in thalamum, sponsarum more, coruscum

Duci, permaneo virgo sine sorde pudica.
Cui debebo fidem soli servare perennem:
Ipsi me toto cordis conamine credo

When I will come to love him secretly,
Then I will know sweetness and shame.
He'll lead me to a bed of tenderness,
I will arise in blood and weakness.
And I will save myself for him alone,
And give myself to him, believing in him.

When I will come to love him secretly,
He will not cause me shame.
He'll lead me to a bed of tenderness,
I will arise a maiden deep in love.
And I will save myself for him alone,
And give myself to him, believing in him.

If I but could, if I but could,
I'd save you, I'd save you,
But darkness thickens.
There's no letter, name, or count to the gray sea.
It wavers once. It wavers twice.
Respond to me across the seas,
Am I alive or dead.
Does my voice find you where it seeks
Or is there only emptiness?
Respond to me across the seas – what am I now?
What am I now to you?
The same one still, or not?
A sister, or a trait
Of the horizon?

The shadows of the herds fly home.
There awaits my desired one.
The desired long-awaited greedy one awaits
Asleep in the damp earth.
Sprouts to the heavens!
He's free, gigantic,
Across him oxen roam and the clouds run.
His dark eyes are
Hotter than fiery fryers
And his frightful hand is gentler than a child's.

He is my home
The kind of place
Where the dead sit
Silently staring at the fire
He is my home,
Into which step
I, an unmarried bride.
And kiss his palm,
Only the palm.

Your father lies crushed by the sea's weight
He is the volume of the wave, the coral.
Your father circles round, diluted by the sea wind
His skin is bark
Acrawl with panicked ants.
The whites of his eyes – prideful pearls.
The yolks of his eyes – worthless pearls.
His skull is a chorale.
Everything in him knells and trembles.
Nothing within him fades,
But everything transforms
Into something strange, thick, promising.
Curious Nereids immerse themselves in this solution –
So as to watch your father's transformations,

Since nothing in him fades, but rather turns
Into you, to you, Ferdinand: your father lives!

Your father sleeps.
Your father is a red
Ball,
Washed up beneath Pont Neuf.
Your father is shame.
He is the heat
of blindness that encroaches when I look at him: the membrane melts.
He is the cold of stammering that like a stinger creeps out of the mouth.

Your father still lives, but he's dozing off.
Look at the sleeper, Ferdinand.
A streamlet of saliva trickles down his chin.

That is the way a canny snake descends a cliff,
The way a fat chain spills into a skiff.

He sighs, not on the outside, somehow – but within:
He'd rather trap the sound inside himself than share it with us:

He's sleeping, Ferdinand. Ice flickers on his curtal lip.
Breath is a very tiny thing, rounded by dreams.

Demeter.
     Hades.
          Persephone.

Demeter, with her head propped on her hand,
Sat on the porch.
       She sorted
The blind manure of last year's spuds.
The July agony presaged
Stillness and drought and ease.
Her child, a pampered youth,
Adored by animals and servants,
Sniffed at the rapid stream
And lacy cloud of pollen.

    Their feelings were rolled up into a ball,
    And time grew over them inside a chest.
    The habit of shaving the pubis in the bath,
    Of being truly grateful to nature
    For russula, for cepe,
    And of mimicking the line of fate.

They aren't bound by the umbilical, but by
Another heavy force of past deception.
The ill moth beats its wings in vain –
A nighttime, putrefying wound.

    The mist will not diffuse
    Within the brain's black cell.
    The music box where Charon dozes
    Is patched with leftovers

From Cerberus's table
Instead of wood wax.
The wheeze, the whisper, and the squawk of crows –
Is a divine transmitter.

After the feast,
A feast awaits the flies.
These are the basements of the world,
This is the world beyond.
A pinkish pearl between white,
Long eyelashes. A sob.
A sharp bend of the neck.
The goblet soon will chill
With multi-colored wines.
A hairy hand's stump lies
Among the peaches, olives.
The marshal of transparent armies,
The martyr of washed-out togas,
Drank up a sip of lustiness
Inside his barracks.

Heavenly love is deaf and dumb,
And empty as a letter's end.
"Oh, Persephone – a milky stream!
Oh, Persephone – a winter dawn!
I tore my heart in madness
Against this cup's sharp edges."

A kitten with a ringlet on its side
Is crushed against a stone by a wild wind.
The Thunderer's shuddering hand
Streaks lightning bolts across the sky.
Amid the shameless howling of the depths, the ocean,
Amid the thickened shimmer of the blue-gray fog
The trace of a catastrophe detracts

From the bewildered plaudits of the waters.
The maiden has vanished. Her cry is dissolved
Inside the glass of an indifferent landscape,
And seaweed's gentle woolen yarn
Has bound the mainland like a bandage.

  Finished with chopping up tomatoes, onions, dill,
  Demeter came out to the porch to call
  Persephone to dinner. The yellow term
  Of grass mowed in July.
  Pernicious gadflies wearing Aztec masks.
  The rooster, having crowed distractedly,
  Entered the roost.
    Where are you, Persephone?
  Roll-call of dreamy stars,
  Black magic of cicadas.
  The young-boy-waterfall
  Harries the grumpy bridge.
  The mother wildly weeps
  In burdock by the road.
  She wakes the dizzied birds,
  Hinders our sleep.
  Tomorrow is a new day,
  Work awaits us.
  What does this shadow seek here,
  Whom does she call?
  The world, so homely-small,
  Is cradled by indifference.
  People sleep and gods sleep
  In the paws of blankets.

The hangover of loneliness approaches
Together with the whitish sniffle of an awkward dawn.
All that, throughout the night, seemed inconsolable,
Becomes, now, squat and miserable.

Demeter licks crumbs off her hand,
The blessed traces of her recollections,
And lightly laughs at midnight hopes.
"You are unable, gods of Greece, to help me.
And not because I didn't guard my daughter:
Kinship's obsessive. Weakness – that's the ghost
That hinders me from dozing off and sleeping.
Besides, it constantly gnaws at the chest
Close to the nipple. As if drops of blood
Emerged there… "

    The funny play "Fidelity and Love"
    Has flopped again,
    The public hisses tirelessly.
    Down in the pit, Persephone and Hades
    Boast of the bitterness of their resentment,
    Demeter wipes off make-up with a dirty puff.
    You're waiting for an aphorism? There is none.
    A thoughtful, furious divinity
    Sits in the corner, locked in an embrace with chocolate.

I hunted for him in my bed
I hunted but did not find him
I'll walk across the town the streets and squares
The squares the streets across the town
Guards met me, circling the town
How is your loved one better than the other loved ones
His hands are golden cobblestones, beset with topaz
His hands – his rivers, flowing into me
His hands – two lines of verse wound up with rhyme
His hands – dark-watered Neva River and Fontanka
In the ice-stream
With smelt's cucumber-grimy little bodies
And with the acrid breath of palaces on the damp day's surface.

He is all cherries plums and gooseberries
And clumsy bees and caterpillars
He ripens, buzzes, overflows, and shivers,
Romping in inflorescence

His abdomen is like an ivory sculpture
Pitted all over with the pox of pearls

Who is your loved one? He's a gardener
He's – a Garden. He's – en. He's – er. He's – Neither nor.
And his hands are as dark as medicinal mud.

And into this mixture I lower my dismembered body
Neck separately shoulders separately right breast left breast
I am a smelt in untamed water
I am a shell of ice within the ice-stream
I am now as I wished myself to be

Once in my fearsome maidenhood
I am a heavy dirty cluster
Bent down to earth by heaviness, like Samson

Catch us the foxes fox-cubs who have charged into the vineyard
I am a fox-cub who has charged into the vineyard
Catch me with your lips your lips your lips
Just like a grape, my dear, catch me
Squeeze joyous flesh out of the shiny skin onto your tongue
Carry it in your heated larynx
And with the well-like murk of the esophagus
Scare torture tease

Mother please send me a smidgen of money
I'll go and buy myself a basin

Please send me twenty francs
For washing my hands and my forehead.

A fragile porcelain item resembling an udder
for the hour when Paris's prostitutes crawl out of their burrows
And flutter their alarmed allergic nostrils
Anticipating air
The rustle!
The hour when the whole town flutters its mysterious doors.

Money's essential
For washing my hands and forehead of sorrowful sweat.
My work somehow doesn't bring income.

My work is to spy through the window, as, through the back door,
Buildings are penetrated by magic invisible creatures –

Delicate soundless like guinea pigs blubbery backs.
I watch them
Never dreaming of procuring them
There's no such lustiness

I wish to seize them
Just in verse
Just in the poem's dark square room
(where in the corner, dear mother, there could be a basin…)
I know how to have and to know their tidy warm shadows
From which I would like to wash myself right after
Shadows of monstrous fish upon the iridescent membrane of the sea

Oh dear mother how dirty I am
I haven't washed I've stayed a dirty scamp
Mornings and evenings oh for shame for shame

Nights:
I sink into a sloop
siren-fish slip along the sides
They shout out in a drawl: clearly
they call me – twenty francs twenty francs

For Katia Kapovich

2.

Learn to be meek. Learn not to be.
Learn to be absent – these kinds of things.
Don't howl, apostate, for sweet mist,
For city noise, go feed your family,
At night, under your seven veils,
Dream that the Baptist rolls your head
Along the track toward the house.
Along the vodka stalls and ragged flower beds,
The pleasantly befouled gazebos,
Just like Columbus lost at sea,
The Baptist – my conceited dialogist –
Pushes the clod, impales the head-
Ing of a chapter final in its meaning.
He's seized my words just as the night-
Time shadow of an owl seizes a rat.

I am a rat out of Columbus's thigh,
Out of the Baptist's lips, I'm gray on gray.
I'm misfortune ripped out with a scalpel,
And the city, with its vaunted body,
Burns and teases me – it's never bright.

Herodias's strained neck bends
Toward me, shame's saliva breaks
Out of her mouth just like a snake:
Teach yourself doubt, dear Salome.

3.

The sharpness of the summer's first half,
The finical duality of its second.
How firmly I remember this!
The mangled stripe of light
Struggles against the lilac stripe
Of twilight, and the cigarette
Breaks, soaked with leaden dew.

It's time to sleep: for children, and for beasts,
For spirits of the marshland, and for kings,
Now off to bed, flop down without a peep!
But July's firefly won't sleep.

Why don't you sleep, my little mate,
My little portion of white light?
This once we chanced upon each other,
You and I, here on the earth!
And so we glanced at one another,
As if we had achieved our goal,
Glanced and went off on separate paths.

You took your path upon the air,
Shuddering and limping.
A fidgety and crimping
Line amid black bodies –
Nighttime stains, you are
A dotted line marking to what
Extent this miracle exists!
Marking also where I ought

To go off in hopes of seeing
For just a bit, for just a wink

To know to breathe and to despise
To know to run and to despise

The world along your meek and blinding insights.

4. Le Sang D'un Poete

For man it's the season of things
Made of air of silk of linen
For me it's the season of ticks
Cunning and terribly craven

They want to redden your scalp
Like a Carpathian Count or diva of the Alps,
Like Leni with her ice ax.
You roam beneath a leafy cloak,
And ha – your meeting with a tick
Draws near, as with a succubus
Upon an evening of temptation.....

....

You roam wearing your hat, your cloak,
But know – all your protection is a joke,
In every place and out of every place
It waits, keeps vigil like a Soviet text,
It waits for YOU, it doesn't eat the rest,
It has already washed the dishes
In preparation for the feast, and it is set
To swallow, swelling out, your blood
And be like a balloon
On my black wound
And swim
Above pale skin…

Ardor and verve! (Pagliacci! Futuristi!)
Are seen in it – so the lone wolf Burliuk
(star on his forehead) supercharged his trick,

Elena Guro washed the brushes
And plied the soft palms of her hands,
While David seethed about revenge,
The two-meter tall friend droned
And made a morning detour
Around Karpovka River.

The river's rusty blood
Mixed – gouache – with sunset –
So that the poet's blood would spill
In nineteen thirty.

On Vyborgskaia Side – groaning factory whistles.
Behind the Botanical Garden,
Floats inflate.

A mystifier – a device for flaying the air in the vibrant sickness of a bar.
The red-faced men, glued to their red-hot chairs,
Drift off above their multicolored drinks.
Grand dames with wide deflowered backs
Fritter away their reefers
The adolescents swell with beer.

It is precisely here, on a fore-evening just like this,
That he sat watching as his hangover
Flowed over into fresher drunkenness.
On the veranda, sunset flashed its feathers.

He sat. You sat. Now, sight unseen, we will fulfill
The brotherhood of distance. And now I know full well
What shape your life took in this little corner
Of Massachusetts – and the ringlet
Upon the barmaid's neck makes better sense
Than my addressing you with a familiar "you."

What was he drinking? Whiskey, I suppose,
I drink a blended Riesling
Ringlets of ice in a cheap vino.
The girl of my dreams,
The barmaid, seems not to hurry with the chowder,
With the check, with the saucy smile –
She's melted, it appears.
And he alone, like the Cheshire Cat, floats in the air and, with a freckled
        paw,
Keeps wagging: draw up closer. The Riesling clangs and gurgles. Pure
        heaven –
All the same.

Alright, I'll draw up closer – for example, to your photograph painted by
        Liebling, in Holyoke,
In the library with the gargoyles: the cheap sweater is completely crumpled,
A look that's joyless and apologetic,
Cheeks that are joyless and completely crumpled –
Not by the wrinkles of a smile, not by the grimace of delight.

More likely from repulsion at the sight: there in the east
Above South Hadley soars the waxwing of the dawn,
The snow, there, has obtained the color of its droppings.
Nearby, the queens of words had lived, and yearning kings had reigned.

A Father Frost by the name of Robert disgorged the aurora borealis
Into a notebook from an opalescent ice-machine-gun:
About the tracks of animals in snow,
About the crimson twigs before the snow comes on.

You looked at this, you read about it, began to yawn, began to spew,

Death, to a denizen of Petersburg, is like an aborigine's bliss –
Dissolution in nature. On the porch, Emily freezes
In rapture over a phallic rusty watering can.
Impatiently, you leaf through an anthology forgotten
Underneath a bench – how will it end?

The same as always: already by Wednesday, by Thursday,
The distinct groan I CAN'T,
A double portion of swill.
The waxwing, reflected, leaves bloody in the snow
A heart that seems to glower – right in the middle of the throat.

END NOTES

TO LEWIS CARROLL: "The merging of the market with the plant 'Electro-power' ": refers to adjacent locations in St. Petersburg, known as Leningrad during the Soviet era.

CEMETERY AT KOMAROVO: Komarovo: a municipal settlement and re-sort near St. Petersburg, on the shore of the Gulf of Finland. Beginning in the 1940s, Komarovo became a colony for leading Russian writers, artists, composers, and in-tellectuals. Its historic cemetery houses the graves of many of these individuals, most notably that of the poet Anna Akhmatova (1889–1966), *née* Gorenko.

FAREWELL TO GERTRUDE: "Because of them, the marble patches gape, / At Komarovo, for example": See note to "Cemetery at Komarovo."

FAREWELL TO CLIO: "Where on Liteyny Avenue's a house – a monument to Roman madams": refers to a major street in St. Petersburg's business district, and the KGB's infamous headquarters, the so-called "Big House".

FAREWELL TO HAMLET: "Outside, snow bubbles like a glass of Veuve Clicquot": The champagne Veuve Clicquot played a large role in popularizing the drink among the Imperial Russian elite. It is famously praised in Aleksandr Pushkin's (1799–1837) novel in verse *Eugene Onegin* (1825–32).

"Someone was rescued just in time by a Lepage": refers to the French gun-smith Jean Lepage's (1779–1822) famous firearm, which also plays a role in Pushkin's *Eugene Onegin*. It is the dueling pistol chosen by the alienated titular character and his young friend, the naive Romantic poet Lensky.

PANTHEON SEQUENCE: in this cycle of poems à clef, Barskova puns on the name of the great Russian poet Aleksandr Pushkin (1799–1837), and employs the conversational, seemingly prosaic, but rigorously formal Classicist style of his lyrics and of his novel in verse *Eugene Onegin* (1825–32).

III. THE POET PESHKIN: "And I? I am a worm-slave": refers to the infa-mous line by Russian poet Gavriil Derzhavin's (1743–1816) ode to *God* (1784), "I'm king – I'm slave – I'm worm – I'm God!" Though Derzhavin falls squarely in the Neo-classical period, his verse is in every sense Baroque and darkly complex, resembling that of the English Metaphysical poets.

"I'm a Chukchi, friend of snows": refers to the Chukchi, the autochthonous population of the Chukchi Peninsula and the northeastern shores of Russian Asia. They were mercilessly denigrated and lambasted as primitives in Soviet humor.

SHE WILL NEVER COME IN FROM THE COLD: this poem's title responds to the Russian Symbolist poet Aleksandr Blok's (1880–1921) short *vers libre* lyric "She Came in from the Cold..." (1908), in which a young woman wielding some kind of elemental power inspires and frustrates the scholarly narrator in the seemingly mundane surroundings of his St. Petersburg flat.

"Carlos threatened the omnivorous Laura": refers to characters from Aleksandr Pushkin's (1799–1837) "little tragedy" in verse *The Stone Guest* (1830) – a frivolous singer and her overly didactic lover.

"he'd devastated, as locusts had the Principality of Kiev / in the *Tale of Bygone Years*, by the way": refers to the *Tale of Bygone Years* (c. 1113), also called the *Primary Chronicle*, a history of Kievan Rus' from about 850 to 1110 – recounting both a plague of locust and attacks by the nomadic Turkic tribe known as the Polovtsy, or the Cumans.

"curly-headed disrober of Anna Gorenko-Gumilev": refers to the Jewish-Italian Modernist painter Amedeo Modigliani (1884–1920), who sketched the Russian poet Anna Akhmatova (*née* Gorenko) in c. 1911, probably in his studio in Paris's Montparnasse.

"the worn-out butterfly-net from Brian Boyd": refers to Brian Boyd (b.1952), an scholar and biographer of the great Russian-American author and inveterate lepidopterist Vladimir Nabokov (1899–1977).

A TRIP TO HOBOKEN: "That senile regret / In the spirit of Afanasii Fet – for fallen youth. And let...": refers to Afanasii Fet (1820–1892), the foremost Russian poet of the second half of the 19th century.

HAPPINESS: "But I'm not Doctor Bormenthal": refers to a character in Mikhail Bulgakov's (1891–1940) science-fiction novella *Heart of a Dog* (1925), in which a medical procedure (the then popular glandular transplant) transforms a sickly, homeless mutt into a human being. The resulting Sharikov, however, is far from the Soviet ideal of the "new man" – rather, he is an abrasive, profane, and violent scoundrel. Old habits die hard. Eventually, Doctor Preobrazhenskii and his protégé Doctor Bormenthal are forced to reverse the procedure and return Sharikov to his natural state.

POTTERY/POETRY: "But if (hello M. B.!) there is an Up above and Down below": the M. B. in question is the Russian philosopher and literary theorist Mikhail Bakhtin (1895–1975), whose notion of the *carnivalesque* as a liminal zone that is neither here nor there rests on such binary oppositions as *living / dead*, *worldly / non-worldly*, *inside / outside*, and *up / down*.

M A D R E   S E L V A : "Tartu semiotics": refers to a school of Soviet-era cultural and literary semioticians that congregated at the University of Tartu in Estonia and in Moscow. The school's members included Iurii Lotman (1922–93), Vladimir Toporov (1928–2005), and Viacheslav Ivanov (b. 1929).

"Saransk heroics": refers the Russian philosopher and literary theorist Mikhail Bakhtin (1895–1975), who taught at the Mordovian National Pedagogical Institute in Saransk in 1936–7, and gain from 1945 to 1969.

A B A B O O N ' S W I D O W : "The *akyn* / Of the zoo staff": *akyn* refers to a class of traditional Kazakh and Kirghiz improvising poets.

"As Sologub, in empty Petrograd, awaited the ice-out": refers to the Symbolist poet and novelist Fedor Sologub (1863–1927), *né* Teternikov. Sologub lived most of his life in St. Petersburg, or Petrograd. His wife Anastasia's suicide in 1921 was the defining tragedy of his life. Anastasia, distraught over her and her husband's uncertain prospects in the wake of the Revolution, jumped off Tuchkov Bridge and drowned in the Zhdanovka River.

T A K E M Y H E A D I N Y O U R H A N D S : "on Bornholm Island the cat's eye of transgressive / love studied us": refers to Nikolay Karamzin's (1766–1826) tale *The Island of Bornholm* (1795). Among his countless other contributions, Karamzin virtually single-handedly introduced Gothic and Sentimentalist modes and genres into Russian literary discourse, thereby paving the way for Romanticism. *The Island of Bornholm* – with its traveling narrator, its Danish setting, its tragic love affair recounted in song, its castle, and its damsel in distress – is a virtual catalog of Gothic and Sentimentalist tropes. Though, in true Sentimentalist fashion, the nature of the tale's underlying tragedy remains unspoken, a Gothic shadow of incest hangs over the island.

"well, where have you got that Liapkin-Tiapkin?": echoes a question posed in Nikolai Gogol's (1809–52) comedy *The Inspector General* (1836), which revolves around a case of mistaken identity and imposture. A provincial mayor learns of an impending visit by an inspector general from St. Petersburg, traveling incognito. The mayor fears the Inspector will discover the ineptitude of the town's administrators, including the judge Lyapkin-Tyapkin, who's turned his court's hallway into a makeshift poultry farm.

T H E N E W I L I A D : "And, like Zoshchenko, drink mustard gas": refers to the inimitable Soviet-era humorist Mikhail Zoshchenko (1895–1958), whose stories satirized the character of the "proletarian writer". This character was promised – but never quite delivered – by the burgeoning Soviet regime. Zoshchenko was exposed to mustard gas while serving in World War I; for the remainder of his days, his skin bore a yellow tint.

"Derptskii pearls – a yellow earring": refers to Derptskii Lane in St. Petersburg.

"Hail Malchish, of course": refers to the enduring refrain of the Socialist Realist fairy tale, "The Tale of the Military Secret" (1935), penned by the Soviet children's writer Arkadii Gaidar (1904–41), *né* Golikov. Its hero, Malchish-Kibalchish, manages to guard the Red Army's supposed Military Secret in the face of torture and death. Malchish loses his life to the Bourgeouins, but receives a hero's burial by the liberating troops. Steamships, locomotives, pilots, and pioneers pass his grave and everyone exclaims, "Hail Malchish!"

WAR: the italicized quatrains are excerpted and newly translated from the work of the great Russian poet Aleksandr Pushkin (1799–1837).

"*It's not in vain I dreamt you all...*": drawn from Pushkin's sequence "Imitations from the Koran" (1824). This passage, which also alludes to *1 Samuel* (*1 Kings*), is often interpreted as a veiled prediction of the Decembrist Revolt of 1825, led by some of Pushkin's radical friends in the Imperial officer corps.

"*Awake, oh timid one!..*": also drawn from "Imitations from the Koran".

"*But I fear: that midst the clashes...*": drawn from Pushkin's "From Hafiz" (1829), which, despite its title, is neither a translation nor a paraphrase of any of the Persian bard's (1315–90) lyrics.

I EXAMINE MY WEDDING DRESS: "Vrubel's Swan Princess, hung up by her wings": refers to the Russian Symbolist painter, Mikhail Vrubel (1856–1910), and his rendering of a Russian fairy tale motif, *The Swan Princess* (1900). His wife, the famed coloratura soprana Nadezhda Zabela-Vrubel (1868–1913), served as the model for the painting.

"Bushes of fireworks of a Michurin splendor": this image compares a fireworks display to one of the botanical wonders produced by the pioneering Russian geneticist Ivan Michurin (1855–1935).

"(As Blok loved)": refers to the Russian Symbolist poet Aleksandr Blok (1880–1921), who immortalized a French fireworks display in his lyric "Out of thin air – a dark blue fountain" (1913).

VERSES ABOUT THE TIME I WASHED ERIC'S HAIR AND FOAM GOT IN HIS EAR: this poem incorporates and plays variations on themes drawn from M(ikhail) L(eonidovich) Lozinskii's (1886–1955) Russian translation of Shakespeare's *Hamlet* (c. 1599–1601). In large part, the poem is a tribute to Lozinskii's magnificent translation.

"O king of forests!": This refers to Johann Wolfgang von Goethe's (1749-1832) ballad "Der Erlkönig" (1782), which served as the basis for Franz Schubert's (1797–1828) popular *lied*. Vasilii Zhukovskii (1783–1852), Russia's greatest translator of the Romantic era, famously rendered the poem as "The Forest King."

MOTHERHOOD AND CHILDHOOD: as the subtitle indicates, this poem is set in Prague, and is sparked by the contents of Vladimir Nabokov's (1899–1977) *sui generis* memoir, *Speak, Memory* (1951). After his father's murder, Nabokov's sister and mother, Elena Nabokova, *née* Rukavishnikova, settled in Prague; Elena Nabokova passed away there in 1939.

THE ZOO IN WINTER: Frosya: the poet's daughter.

"And VN's Dobuzhinskii caves": refers to the Russian-Lithuanian painter Mstislav Dobuzhinskii (1875–1957), best known for his stark, expressionistic cityscapes. The young VN, or Vladimir Nabokov, was one of his pupils; in *Speak, Memory*, Nabokov recalls that the artist "made [him] depict from memory, in the greatest possible detail, objects [he] had certainly seen thousands of times without visualizing them properly".

MADENESS (URBAN TABLEAUX): this sequence concerns the life and art of the extraordinary Russian "analytical realist" painter, theorist, and Futurist poet, Pavel Filonov (1883–1941), or "*Ph*". His avant-garde approach, referred to as *madeness*, called for building up a large painting up from small, interwoven, interlaced details. His art soon fell out of favor with the Soviet regime, and, refusing to sell his paintings to private collectors, he essentially starved from the early 1930s to the time of his death during the Siege of Leningrad.

Ekaterina Semenovna \ Ekaterina Alexandrovna: refers to the artist's wife. The details recounted in the "Explanatory Preface" are based on actual events.

Glebova, First: refers to the artist's sister, Evdokiia Glebova (1888–1980), who dragged his and his wife's bodies to the cemetery on a sled. Evdokiia preserved the artist's paintings until the 1960s, when exhibitions of the his work were again permitted.

Glebova, Second: refers to Tatiana Glebova (1900–85), who was a remarkable artist in her own right, and Filonov's favorite disciple. She inventively developed the artist's idea of *madeness* after his death.

"Of the Queen of Spades – the two-faced duchess, / Stripping before Hermann": refers to Aleksandr Pushkin's (1799–1837) short story, "The Queen of Spades" (1833).

LOVE VERSES ABOUT PRO-MOTION: "Behind Zhuchka: the granddaughter": refers to the rhyming refrain of the popular Russian folk tale, "The Turnip", in which it takes an entire household tugging in unison – grandfather, grandmother, granddaughter, Zhuchka the dog, the cat, and finally the mouse – to pull an enormous turnip out of the ground.

SCENE: "Soars a bird right out of Blok, a captain out of Gumilev": refers to two great Russian poets of the Silver Age. Birds played a prominent role in Aleksandr

Blok's (1880–1921) Symbolist poems, which include lyrics like "Gamaiun, the Prophetic Bird" (1899) and the verse epic *Nightingale Garden* (1915). The Acmeist Nikolai Gumilev (1886–1921), on the other hand, is known for his markedly masculine poems of war and exotic adventure. He served as a cavalryman in World War I and was unhappily married to his fellow Acmeist Anna Akhmatova (1889–1966). Both poets died in the midst of the Civil War – the first of illness and starvation, and the second of an executioner's bullet. Their deaths marked the end of the Silver Age.

CONJUNCTIVITIS: "The right eyelid won't lift: Salute to Vii!": refers to the titular King of Gnomes in Nikolai Gogol's (1809–52) atmospheric and disturbing horror tale "Vii", which first appeared in his collection *Mirgorod* (1835). Vii's eyelids reach down to the floor.

"Like the enticing micas / Of Bazhov's tales": refers to the fairy tales of the Soviet author Pavel Bazhov (1879–1950), whose collection *The Malachite Casket* (1939) drew heavily on the folklore of the Ural Mountains, where he was born and raised. The composer Sergei Prokofiev (1891–1953) based his final ballet, *The Tale of the Stone Flower*, on Bazhov's tales.

"Like that wag Griboedov": refers to the Russian playwright Aleksandr Griboedov (1795–1829), whose masterpiece, the verse comedy *Woe from Wit* (1823), gave rise to countless "winged words" that have found a permanent nest in the Russians' collective consciousness.

THE BALLAD OF VIKTOR SHKLOVSKII: this poem concerns the literal and literary exploits of the colorful and ingenious Soviet author, critic, and Formalist theoretician Viktor Shklovskii (1893–1984), who served as a Red Army Commissar during the Civil War.

VARIATIONS ON A THEME II: this poem re-casts and re-acts to the Polish poet Konstanty Ildefons Gałczyński's (1905–53) phantasmagoric sequence "The Enchanted Carriage" (1948), itself inspired by Kraków's famous Horse Cabs. The characters are drawn from Gałczyński's poem, while the place names – the Old Town Square, the Vistula River, Podgórski Market Square, and Lwowska Street – are all Krakowian.

WINTER TALES: "Like Rozanov's wondrous fluids from a beauty's marvelous body": refers to the Russian philosopher and author Vasilii Rozanov (1856–1919), whose attempts to reconcile the Russian religious tradition with a joyous embrace of sexual desire proved a scandal in the late-19th and early-20th centuries.

AFFECTU QUEM SECRETO: this poem takes as its inspiration and adapts the work of the German Benedictine canoness and poet Hrotsvitha (c. 935 to c. 1002).

The Latin portion is a passage from the poet's book *Agnes*, one of the "Legends": "When I love him in the inmost affection of my heart, no loss do I suffer of maidenhood; but when I merit the joy of His embrace and like a bride am led to His glorious bridal-chamber, I remain a virgin without violation of chastity." (Tr. Sister M. Gonsalva Wiegand, *The Non-Dramatic Works of Hrosvitha. Text, Translation, and Commentary* [Saint Louis, MO: Saint Louis U, 1936], 243.)

DEDICATION 4. LETTER TO MOTHER FROM CHARLES B.: this poem is framed as a letter from the French Romantic/Symbolist poet and critic Charles Baudelaire (1821–67) to his mother.

DOBYCHIN IN BRIANSK SEQUENCE: this sequence is built around figure of the Russian Modernist author Leonid Dobychin (1896–1936), who committed suicide shortly after the publication of his stylistically innovative short novel *The Town of N* (1935). Dobychin spent the period from 1918 to 1927 in the Russian town of Briansk, sharing a crowded room with several relatives.

4. LE SANG D'UN POETE: "the lone wolf Burliuk": refers to the Ukrainian-born Futurist artist, illustrator, designer, and author David Burliuk (1882–1967), who fled the Soviet Union in 1918, and died in the United States.

"Elena Guro washed the brushes": refers to the little-known but significant Russian Impressionist, proto-Futurist author and painter Elena Guro (1877–1913).

"So that the poet's blood would spill / In nineteen thirty": refers to the suicide of the great Russian poet and artist Vladimir Maiakovskii (1893–1930).

AN EXTRAORDINARY ADVENTURE OCCURRING LAST SUMMER IN SOUTH HADLEY: this poem imagines an encounter with the Russian-American poet Joseph Brodsky (1940–1996). After his exile from the Soviet Union in 1972, Brodsky taught for fifteen years at Mount Holyoke College in South Hadley, Massachusetts. Jerome Liebling's (b. 1924) photograph of the poet now hangs in the college library.